TEXTILE MANUFACTURERS' BOOK-KEEPING F HOUSE, MILL AND WAREHOUSE • GEORGE PE

Publisher's Note

The book descriptions we ask booksellers to display prominently warn that this is an historic book with numerous typos or missing text; it is not indexed or illustrated.

The book was created using optical character recognition software. The software is 99 percent accurate if the book is in good condition. However, we do understand that even one percent can be an annoying number of typos! And sometimes all or part of a page may be missing from our copy of the book. Or the paper may be so discolored from age that it is difficult to read. We apologize and gratefully acknowledge Google's assistance.

After we re-typeset and design a book, the page numbers change so the old index and table of contents no longer work. Therefore, we often remove them; otherwise, please ignore them.

Our books sell so few copies that you would have to pay hundreds of dollars to cover the cost of our proof reading and fixing the typos, missing text and index. Instead we let most customers download a free copy of the original typo-free scanned book. Simply enter the barcode number from the back cover of the paperback in the Free Book form at www.RareBooksClub.com. You may also qualify for a free trial membership in our book club to download up to four books for free. Simply enter the barcode number from the back cover onto the membership form on our home page. The book club entitles you to select from more than a million books at no additional charge. Simply enter the title or subject onto the search form to find the books.

If you have any questions, could you please be so kind as to consult our Frequently Asked Questions page at www.RareBooksClub.com/faqs.cfm? You are also welcome to contact us there.

General Books LLC™, Memphis, USA, 2012.

❧ ❧ ❧ ❧ ❧ ❧ ❧ ❧

LIBRARY OF ALLEN KNIGHT CERTIFIED PUBLIC ACCOUNTANT 502 California Street SAN FRANCISCO. CALIFORNIA EXTRACTS FROM PRESS NOTICES.

"One of the best treatises we have seen, certainly the best we have reviewed for some years. It has been specially designed for the Woollen and Worsted trade and should take rank as the Standard Work on Book-keeping and Accounts in such business... Remarkable for its technical accuracy."—*The Accountant,* June 29th, 1889.

"Mr. Norton has provided a text book, not merely of undoubted merit, but which will be recognised as an authority. He shows that he is thoroughly acquainted with all, even the minuteat details of a textile manufacturer's business Nothing appears to have escaped notice, and every transaction is explained and illustrated by an example... . Altogether this book is the most Complete work on the subject that has issued from the press and yet exceedingly simple, excluding everything that tends to increase the labour of the counting house without any corresponding value. "—*Textile Recorder.*

"This work is in every sense of a thoroughly practical character clear, concise comprehensive. Words of ours cannot express what is due to the anthor for the *admirable way in which he has put before manufacturers generally a true system of book-keeping...* easily comprehended.... The Appendix gives a fund of practical information.... The work ought to be in the hands of every manufacturer." *Journal of Fabrics and Textile Industries.*

Fob Further Extracts See Prospectus.
MANUFACTURERS' BOOK-KEEPING FOR THE COUNTING HOUSE, MILL AND WAREHOUSE.
BEING A PRACTICAL TREATISE, SPECIALLY DESIGNED FOR THE WOOLLEN AND WORSTED AND ALLIED TRADES.
BY
GEORGE PEPLER NORTON, F.C.A., CHARTERED ACCOUNTANT,
(AUTHOR OF "BALANCING FOR EXPERT BOOK-KEl-PERS," ETC.: PRIZEMAN FINAL EXAMINATION OF THE INSTITUTE OF CHARTERED ACCOUNTANTS, JUNE, 1ss3),
OF THE FIRM OF
ARMITAGE & NORTON,
OF HUDDERSFIELD, BRADFORD AND DEWSBURY.
FOURTH EDITION.
1 9oo.

London: Simpkin, Marshall, Hamilton, Kent & Co., Limited.
Manchester: Emmott & Co., New Bridge Street.
Bradford: Brear & Co., Limited, Kirkgate.
Edinburgh & Glasgow: John Menzies & Co.

First Edition...... Jan, 1889.
Second Edition April, 1891.
Third Edition October, 1894.
Fourth Edition July, 19oo.

PREFACE TO THE THIRD EDITION.
The previous editions have been carefully revised and in many minor matters improved, but substantially the structure of the book is unchanged.

The utility of the system of Bookkeeping which the book explains has been confirmed by the experience of nearly six years' working in very varied circumstances since the publication of the first edition.

The Author has had the gratification of finding, in numerous instances, that the book has been utilised in trades widely different from those for which it is specially designed; and the large number of letters which he has received relating to questions of detail prove that the book has been carefully studied and that its teaching has been intelligently applied.

GEO. P. NORTON. *Huddcrsfield, Octo-*

ber, 1894. 380304 PREFACE TO THE SECOND EDITION.

Since the publication of the first edition of this work in 1889, six hundred copies have passed into the hands of manufacturers in Great Britain, the Colonies, the United States of America, Germany and other foreign centres of the textile industries.

The system of book-keeping which the book describes is now very generally adopted, and I have found no reason for altering the original text.

In order that those who intend to adopt the system may have properly designed books, I have arranged with the printer, Mr. Alfred Jubb, Huddersfield, to supply books to approved patterns and at fixed prices.

GEO. P. NORTON. *Huddersfield, April,* 1891. PREFACE.

The appearance of the present treatise, adding to the already numerous publications on the subject of book-keeping, may be thought to require some explanation.

It will perhaps be sufficient to say, that this volume is devoted to a special industry, and that its design is essentially different from that of other works. The reason for its appearance has arisen out of the peculiar relations of my firm to the manufacturing industries. A large audit practice amongst manufacturers in all parts of the kingdom has rendered almost necessary the production, in some shape, of a comprehensive guide for their book-keepers. My primary intention was to prepare printed instructions that might be referred to in cases of difficulty, but constant evidence of the insufficiency of fragmentary instructions ultimately developed the idea of publishing a complete treatise.

Circumstances have greatly favoured me by providing the amplest facilities for gathering all requisite information. The Chambers of Commerce of Leeds, Huddersfield and Dewsbury in 1879 established the Creditors Association of Manufacturers, and appointed my firm as Accountants to the Association. This, and a similar appointment held from the Home Merchants, in addition to a general practice, has brought under my firm's control many insolvencies both at home and abroad. Opportunities have therefore been forthcoming for inspecting the accounts of traders in every branch of textile fabric manufacture, of their agencies and branches in all parts of the world, and of the Merchants with whom they deal.

In advising as to causes of failure, decrease of profits, and the results of trading, I have had constantly to investigate, not only into the financial books, but also into those connected with the Mill, Factory and Warehouse. To do this effectually, it has been necessary to acquaint myself with much purely technical information as to the processes of manufacture, and the modus operandi of production and distribution. This extra-professional knowledge has proved very helpful in preparing this work.

I have for several years sought with much diligence to rectify the defects of prevailing systems, and at the same time have carefully selected from them those forms which practical experience and long usage have proved to be the fittest. I have endeavoured to retain what is essential and to discard all that is superfluous, avoiding, as far as possible, all repetition and re-copying of entries. My chief aim has been to obtain everywhere accuracy, lucidity, and completeness by the shortest possible process.

To practical observation I have added a thorough and exhaustive study of what has been previously written upon the theory of book-keeping.

I might perhaps venture to lay claim to certain improvements adapted to all classes of wholesale business, but I prefer to send forth this treatise as an exposition of the best methods that obtain in the manufacturing industries, and of a system that is in successful operation in many of the largest manufacturing concerns in the textile fabric trades.

I can scarcely hope to have provided for all the multifarious requirements of an industry which is so extensive and varied, and must crave the indulgence of my readers for any shortcomings. In extenuation of minor errors or omissions I may plead that my time has been so much occupied with other pressing duties.

In conclusion I have to express my sincere thanks to several friends, who, being manufacturers in various trades, have so kindly given me their assistance and practical advice.

G. P. NORTON.

Huddersfield, January, 2889.

Chapter II.—ELEMENTARY PRINCIPLES ILLUSTRATED—

Opening Books—Accounts of Property as a *whole,* and of its several *partt*

Treatment of a series of ordinary business transactions

Trial Balance

Trading Account, Capital Account, and Balance Sheet

Specimen Accounts

Classification of transactions in separate books of entry—Journal

Chapter III.—MANUFACTURER'S BOOKS, SET I: SIMPLE TRANSACTIONS

List of commencing Balances and Balance Sheet..

List of Books employed

Purchases Day Book.... Example Pages 29, 30, Description

Returns And Claims (purchases)

Chapter IV.—MANUFACTURER'S BOOKS, SET II.: comprising all classes of transactions connected with textile manufacturing

Purchases Day Book (with classification columns)

..Example pages 82—93, Description 198

Returns And Claims (purchases) Day Book

Mill Sales Day Book

Sales Day Book, Pattern Day Book

Returns And Allowances (sales) Day Book

Cash Book

(with columns classifying the entries according to the Ledgers to which they are posted)

Purchases Or Mill Ledger

Sales Ledger

Bills Ledgers

(Payable and Recivable)

Nominal Ledger

Balance Book

Test Journal
Private Ledger
(including Capital Accounts,
 List of Final Balances,
 Trading Account specially arranged, and Balance Sheet)
DEPARTMENTAL ACCOUNTS—
 Selling Departments..
 Manufacturing Departments..
 Volume And Value Ok Production And Decimal Calculations
 Chapter V.—SPECIAL AND AUXILIARY BOOKS—
 Goods Received Book—Goods Delivered Book—Delivery Note Book 227
 Detail Ledger—Tare Records........ 228, 229
 Sales Ledger for Seasons' Goods....... . 230, 231
 Another form of Cash Book.......... 231, 232
 Chapter VI.—DEPRECIATION-
Buildings—Leases—Plant and Machinery—Cards—Depreciation Table
 Chapter VII.—FINANCE AND DUTIES OF THE CASHIER—
 Manipulation of Capital—Banking—Discounting—Bills—Outstanding and overdue Accounts, Ac....... 238—240
 Chapter VIII.—WAGES—
 A complete system described—Pay Tickets, Tables and Boxes—
 Departmental Summary—Tests of results of labour—Collusion
 —Workpeoples' Record—Piecework Record—Timeworkers—
 Metallic Check System—Forms........ 241—246
PAGE
 Chapter IX.—MILL OR FACTORY AND WAREHOUSE BOOKS—
 Order Book at Mill for Purchases....... .. 247
 Stock And Cost Books for Purchases, viz:—
 Raw Materials...... Description page 248, Form 262
 Yarn—Dyewares, Chemicals, Soap, Oil, Ac.—Mill Furnishings and Loose Utensils.. ,, 249 ,, 262, 263
 Stock And Cost Books relating to the processes of manufacture, viz: —
 Woollen Yarn—Combing, or Tops.. „ 260 „ 263,264
 Worsted Yarn.... ,, 261 266
 Piece Order Book at Mill.. „ 261 „ 266
 Orders Making Classification Book.,, 262,, 260, 267
 Yarn Shade Register.... „ 262 „ 268
 Weaver's Ticket—Ptece Making Or Balk Book...... „ 263 „ 266—268
 Piece Cost Book—Warehouse Order Book........ „ 264 269, 270
 Warehouse Stock Book —consignment
 Stock Books...... „ 266 270,271
 Records Ok Work In Departments.. „ 260, 267
 Summary Of Work Done and periodical Statement of *Machinery* or *Manufacturing Profit or Losa..* „ 268,, 271
 Stocktaking............ 269, 200
APPENDIX.
 I.—Alphabetical Index to Ledger: Vowel System.... 274, 276
 II.—Different Methods of preparing a Trial Balance.... 276, 277
 III. —Interest Calculations.......... 277, 278
 IV. —How to discover and avoid Common Errors...... 278 — 280
 V.—The Advantages of a Professional Audit...... 280, 281
 VI.—Income Tax............ 281—286
 VII.—Bills of Exchange, Promissory Notes, Cheques, and Letters of Credit............ 286-294
 VIII.—Information on Mercantile Subjects, viz:
 Bills of Lading............ 294
 Guaranty and Collateral Security—Interest—Lien—Statute of Frands, Contracts over £10........ 296
 Statutes of Limitation—Stoppage *in Transitu*.... 296
INDEX 297—300
INTRODUCTION.

It is no part of my present intention to enlarge upon the origin and history of book-keeping by double-entry, as to which the curious or inquisitive reader may consult many writers who have treated the subject generally. Suffice it to say that various conjectures have been put forward which ascribe to this common-place practical science a descent dating as far back as the commencement of the christian era. Like most other useful arts it has developed gradually, advancing step by step with commerce and civilisation. Lucas di Borgo, a friar and mathematician, was the author of what is supposed to be the first treatise on the subject. His work was published in the Italian language at Venice in 1494-5. Since that date numerous publications have appeared, putting forward different ideas of more or less interest, but the general theory of the so-called Italian system has never yet been successfully assailed. Its fundamental principles remain, although the changes of time, the progress and extension of trade and its manifold ramifications, have necessitated a variety of modifications in practice.

The writers of a few modern treatises have with much skill and lucidity explained the science or general laws of book-keeping, and have in fact left very little to be desired in that direction. The method of exposition usually adopted has been to state, and str6ngly emphasize the general propositions of the science, and to apply them to particular cases by means of a few brief examples. Furthermore, the writers have, almost invariably, proceeded on the assumption that every difficulty can be surmounted by those who have committed to memory the formulas and rules. It would be accounted unreasonable to expect an apprentice to be competent to design and weave, because he had learned that to construct a piece of cloth he must pass the threads of the weft transversely through those of the warp. Nevertheless, to know that " every debit must have a corresponding credit" is the equivalent in book-keeping to such a knowledge of cloth construction. In the one case it is required to place an infinite variety of transactions in their proper accounts, and in the other to place a diversity of threads of yarn in their proper position. Formulas and rules afford very little guidance in such matters, which can only be made intelligible through a primary experimental acquaintance with the details of actual practice.

Following the text books, most teachers of book-keeping have ineffectually conveyed confused ideas of abstract theory to the minds of their students, who in the majority of cases, have promptly forgotten them. It is, therefore, not surprising that so many traders, thus taught at school, should regard double-entry book-keeping with prejudice and disfavour (a).

Although the principle of double-entry book-keeping is said to be deduced from the mathematical axiom, that "the whole is equal to the sum of the parts," in my opinion the invention of the system is to be ascribed rather to induction than to deduction. Book-keeping was practised long before its formulas and rules were even thought of: ancient traders did not wait until a scientific system had been constructed to record their business transactions. The science was evolved out of, and was organised after, practice, and it is only in this order that it can be taught. Herbert Spencer remarks that, "Every science is evolved out of its corresponding art: there must be practice and accruing experience before there can be science." And it will be found that this natural principle is followed in the succeeding pages. Details, and the practical application of the art, receive paramount attention, and progress is made by easy gradations from the simple to the complex. Nevertheless, the functions and importance of the science are recognised, and it is fully explained at the outset, in order to help the memory and assist the reason whilst the student is step by step acquiring a mastery over the details of the art.

The reader will doubtless be familiar with the phrase, " Bookkeeping by Single-entry,'' and may possibly have conceived a bias in favour of a practice bearing so attractive a title. To offer any explanation of what is generally understood by "single-entry," would *(a)* The want ot thorough teaching on this subject is becoming more strongly felt by trading communities, and, to supply the want, several large educational establishments have sought professional assistance.

Moreover, apart from its practical application in after life, 1 venture to submit that double-entry book-keeping is deserving of more attention as a means of elementary intellectual discipline. Much of the training given in the abstract sciences loses its hold upon the mind, which is occupied by the symbols used, and often fails to grasp what those symbols stand for. In book-keeping the necessities of numerical relation are demonstrated by illustrations sufficiently interesting to make a lasting impression upon the mind; and how far the practice of book-keeping produces analytical and synthetical habits of mind will be gathered from a careful perusal of these pages.

serve no useful purpose to those for whom this treatise is written. The term bears the same relation to double-entry that chaos does to order, and comprises every style of book-keeping that is imperfect, and unreliable. As a matter of fact, there is not in actual practice, any book-keeping, where a ledger is kept, that is carried on by single-entry.

It may be well here to point out some of the disadvantages of imperfect book-keeping, and to cite a few illustrations from my own experience. In one instance, accounts collected by a partner were systematically embezzled by him, either wholly or in part; the frauds being covered by the manipulation of a rough cash book. Many thousands of pounds were thus abstracted from the partnership funds. Unintentional mis-statements of partners' accounts are very frequent, and in one case a single error of nearly £2,000 was brought to light by subsequent investigation. Payment of the same accounts twice over, and omissions in posting sales to the ledger, are errors of common occurrence. Accounts are often posted wrongly, and, although called over, are still passed without notice *(e.g., £15: 10: o* may be posted as 15s. iod., called over as *fifteen ten,* and passed as correct). In ruling off settled ledger accounts, the line is sometimes drawn beneath items not paid for in the settlement, which are consequently overlooked. The adjustment of the Capital Account, especially in partnership cases, is a very fruitful field for blunders, and I have discovered errors, in some instances, involving thousands of pounds.

Most of the errors above-mentioned would have been prevented by applying the system of double-entry; but it should be understood that the principles of double-entry afford protection only to a limited extent. Serious mistakes often occur in accounts where the system is imperfectly adapted, and in many cases of fraud, where the books have been carefully balanced by double-entry, the system has been so applied, that, instead of revealing, it has concealed the falsification of the accounts. In an extraordinary instance, while investigating the books of a manufacturing firm, balanced by double-entry, an item of more than,£"1,ooo, for the sale of disused machinery, was found entered in the Sales Day book, which had been carried forward and counted as income.

It would be quite easy to adduce many similar cases, from the books of business men, who in other respects are models of forethought and ability.

The amount of money lost, and the frequency of errors that are allowed to pass without ever being observed, solely because of imperfect book-keeping, would astonish any but those who have had considerable experience as auditors. Where the transactions of a business are at all numerous errors will occur more or less frequently, though the book-keeper be ever so skilful.

It is essential, therefore, that the books employed should not only be kept by double-entry, but that they should be well devised, and thoroughly adapted to the particular trade. A clumsy adaptation of double-entry may prove quite as unreliable as single-entry.

In manufacturing concerns, especially, it is of the utmost importance to obtain the very best skill in arranging, adapting, and keeping the books; a fact which is gradually gaining fuller recognition. In the face of daily increasing competition the utmost vigilance is required, and the manufacturer must be able to compare periodically the expenditure and income arising out of each department of his business. The time has gone by for the large margin between the cost and selling prices, when any blunderer with capital could make a profit. *Caterisparibus,* he whose books promptly disclose pertinent information concerning the leading features of his business, will undoubtedly be the most successful. The modern captain of a well-provided vessel does not possess greater advantages over the ancient star-directed mariner, than the manufacturer, with his unfailing scientific system of book-keeping, possesses over his neighbours who are guided by crude and old-world methods. It is equal folly, in either case, to venture both fortune and prospects and court shipwreck, while disregarding the excellent directing appliances provided by modern invention.

After having had ample opportunities for forming a correct judgment, I have no hesitation in affirming that the practice of imperfect book-keeping is the main cause of many failures. It is, moreover, fruitful of much moral evil, both inviting and concealing embezzlement and fraud.

The oft-repeated objection, that double-entry is too intricate for ordinary business men to understand, is solely the outcome of cumbersome and absurd applications of the system. The services of a skilled accountant in opening the books of a new firm, or in remodelling those of an existing business, will be found very helpful, and a specialist in the particular branch of trade should be consulted where convenient.

The principal advantages to be derived from well organised doubleentry book-keeping may be briefly summarised as follows, viz:— 1. The correctness of the book-keeping is tested with absolute certainty.
2. The state of the personal accounts, of both Debtors and

Creditors, can be ascertained instantly.
3. Accounts of Goods bought and sold, of Revenue and Expenditure, of Stock, and other property, are accurately kept.
4. A Balance Sheet, and accounts shewing the working details of the trading, and also of profit and loss resulting therefrom, both as a whole and in departments, are readily prepared. 5. Accounts of partners are kept in such a manner as will prevent fraud, and even the cause for suspicion that frequently exists without foundation in fact. 6. The possibility of fraud by book-keepers and cashiers is re duced, owing to the ample means furnished for scrutiny and detection. CHAPTER I.
Elementary Principles.
The books of every trader ought to show,— 1. The value of his trading property as a *whole,* 2. The value of the several *parts* thereof.

By way of illustration, assume that on January 1st B is possessed of property valued at *£b,ooo,* consisting of Wool,£"5,ooo, and Cash,£"1,ooo.

To record his position, three distinct accounts are opened in his books, viz:—
(i.) Capital Account, which is *credited* with "6,ooo, the value of B's property as a *whole.* (ii.) Wool Account, which is *debited* with the value of one *part,* viz. ,£"5,ooo.
(iii.) Cash Account, which is *debited* with the value of the other *part,* viz. £1,000.
On January 2oth, B purchases more wool, and pays for it in cash *£500.* This transaction affects the two *parts* of B's property, and requires, therefore, to be twice recorded.

In the early days of book-keeping the accounts in B's books might have appeared as follows:—
My Total Property Account, *(i.e. Capital)*
Jan. 1 By value of wool 5,ooo ,, Cash in hand 1,ooo 6,ooo
My Wool Account, (one part)
Jan. 1 To value of wool on hand 5,ooo
,, 20 Add amount purchased for cash 5oo 5.5
My Cash Account, (the other part) £
Jan. 1 To amount of cash on hand 1,ooo
,, 2o Deduct amount paid for wool 5oo 5oo It will be observed that B's Capital, or property as a *whole,* is the same both before, and after, the purchase of wool on January 2oth; the transaction being merely an exchange of *parts* of his property.

Assume further, that because of a fall in the market, on January 3oth, B sells his entire stock of wool for 5,ooo cash, and consequently makes a loss of "5oo.

To record this,,£"5,ooo must be deducted from the Wool Account, and "5,ooo must be added to the Cash Account.

This transaction, however, not only affects the two *parts* of B's property, but also his capital, or property as a *whole,* which is decreased by the loss of /5oo; the /5oo remaining in the Wool Account being of no value.

Therefore, to record the loss, 5oo must be deducted from the Wool Account, and /5oo must also be deducted from the Capital, or total property, Account.

If B were to sell his wool at a profit, and not at a loss, the Wool Account, and the Capital, or total property, Account, would have to be *increased,* instead of decreased.

It follows, therefore, *that every increase or decrease of any part of the property, unless compensated by the like decrease or increase of another part, involves a corresponding increase or decrease of the whole.*

The method of adding or subtracting each transaction, as shown in the previous example, has long since given place to the more convenient plan, by which one side of an account is appropriated to all items of increase, and the other to all items of decrease.

The above-mentioned transactions would now appear in the following form.

The state of an account is ascertained, at any time, by adding each side and comparing the totals.

The sides of an account, thus divided, are technically called *(b)* "debit " and " credit " (usually written " Dr." and " Cr. ")

To *debit* an account is to enter on the *left hand* side, and to *credit* an account is to enter on the *right hand* side.
(b) In the succeeding pages of this book, the abbreviations" Dr." and " Cr." are used instead of the words debit or debtor, and credit or creditor.
Each entry on the "Dr." side is usually

prefaced by the word "To," and each entry on the "Cr." side by the word "By"; implying that the person, or thing, represented by the heading of the account, is Dr. to, or Cr. by, the sum entered.

The expression "Double-entry" aptly describes the governing principle of the system, which requires that every transaction shall be *twice* recorded; to the Dr. of one account in the ledger, and to the Cr. of another.

Consequently, *for every* Dr. *there must be a corresponding* Cr.

The two-fold nature of mercantile dealings will be obvious to all; *e.g.* if a person becomes my debtor, it follows that I become his creditor, or *vice versa (c)*. This duality exists in every kind of business transaction.

In double-entry book-keeping there are three distinct classes *(d)* of accounts, viz:— (i.) *Personal Accounts, i.e.,* accounts of persons dealing with the firm. (ii.) *Property Accounts, e.g..* Machinery, Business Premises, &c. (iii.) *Nominal Accounts, i.e.,* accounts of income, and expenditure, such as Sales Account, Purchases Account, Wages Account, etc.

All classes of accounts are governed by the same fundamental principles. The subjects represented by both the Property Accounts (ii.), and the Nominal Accounts (iii.), are deemed to be *personified*, and are treated as persons; thus, I sell cloth, value £20, to B on credit; in my books B is debited with the price as the receiver, and *Cloth,* is credited as the giver. The entry would be as follows:— (c) In my books the person is Dr. and the thing given to him is Cr.

(d) By different writers accounts have been described and classified in various ways. (Personal, including (i.) For instance-j and (Impersonal, including (ii.) and (iii.)
Personal, including (i.)
Real, including (ii.)
and
Nominal or Fictitious, including (iii.) (Real, including (i.) and (ii.) or and (Fictitious, including (iii.)

Some nice arguments, which it is not necessary to discuss, have been raised concerning both classification and nomenclature. The several views are given so that the reader may be acquainted with the various designations that are in common use.

Cloth Account represents me, and it might be headed My (Cloth) Account, and thus personified.

All the accounts in the ledger may, therefore, be regarded as accounts of persons, that is, either accounts of the trader himself, on the one hand, or of persons with whom he has dealings, on the other.

If this principle be fully recognised, and clearly understood, much of the difficulty in determining whether any item is to be posted to the Dr. or Cr. of an account will be removed.

The account which *receives* is always Dr., and the account which *gives out* is always Cr.

Thus, in the above illustration, B *received* cloth, and is therefore Dr., Cloth Account *gave out* cloth, and is consequently, Cr.

CHAPTER ll.
Elementary Principles Illustrated.
The principles laid down in the foregoing pages, are applied and illustrated in the following specimen accounts.

A series of imaginary transactions, dissimilar in nature, is chosen to represent the most frequent and important classes of mercantile dealings. For the sake of brevity a few items only are selected as examples of each class, and all explanatory details are omitted.

Abraham Crosland, a manufacturer, is supposed to commence the year with capital amounting to *£4,500,* made up as follows:— ASSETS. £ £
Stock of Goods 3,16o
Plant and Machinery 2,2oo
Cash in hand 22o
Owing to him, by Thomas Allen 3,000
Do. George Brownson 2,1oo 5,1oo
Less LIABILITIES, viz:— 1o,68o
Owing by him, to John Blamires 3.45
Do. Albert Lodge 73o
Do. West Yorkshire Bank... 2,000 6,18o
Leaving Surplus or Capital "4,5oo

His transactions during six months are as follows:— £ 1 Purchased goods of John Blamires 3,2oo 2 Sold goods to George Brownson 7,2oo 3 Returned goods (purchased) to Albert Lodge 75 4 Received from George Brownson, cash 6,74o 5 Received from Thomas Allen, acceptance due May 1st, in part payment of his account 2,1oo 6 Paid Albert Lodge, cash 2oo 7 Goods (sold) returned from Thomas Allen 32o 8 Purchased goods of Ephraim Broadbent 2,95o 9 Accepted John Blamires' draft, due June 17th 4,5oo 1o Paid ready-money for purchase of five looms, at auction... 179 1 1 Received from Thomas Allen, cash for his acceptance.. . 2,1oo 12 Sold goods to Thomas Allen 2,8oo 13 Withdrew cash from the West Yorkshire Bank 3,1oo 14 Paid cash to the West Yorkshire Bank 3,32o 15 Paid cash in discharge of my acceptance, due June 17th, to

John Blamires 4,5oo 16 Paid cash for productive Wages 2,7oo 17 Paid cash for Trade Charges 5oo 18 Paid cash for Salaries 24o 19 Paid cash for Rent and Power 25o 20 Paid out of cash for personal expenditure 256

On the principle of double-entry explained on page 6, Abraham Crosland opens in his ledger:— 1. *An account of his property as a whole, entitled* CAPITAL ACCOUNT.

This is really the personal account of Abraham Crosland, who provides the whole surplus capital, or, in other words, is the *giver* (see page 9), and is consequently Cr. for the amount, viz— 4,5oo *(e).* 2. *Accounts of the several parts of his property, viz:—*

Stock Of Goods (,£3,16o), the first item, is posted to the Dr. of the Goods Account. Plant And Machinery Account (,£"2,2oo) and Cash Account (£22o) are Drs. for their respective amounts. These three accounts are treated as though they were persons (see pages 8-9) entrusted with the things they represent, on behalf of Abraham Crosland. He is the *giver,* and therefore the Cr., as shown above, and they are the *receivers,* and therefore the Drs. Thomas Allen (£3,000), and George Brownson (£2,1oo), as *receivers* are Drs. for the amounts owing by them.

Having posted all the assets to the

Dr. of their respective accounts, we now deal with the liabilities, which are, in effect, claims upon, or deductions from, the *parts* of the trader's property.

John Blamires (£3,45o), Albert Lodge (£73o), and the West Yorkshire Bank (£2,ooo) are Crs. for their respective amounts. They are the *givers,* and therefore Crs., and Abraham Crosland, is the *receiver,* and therefore Dr.

Before dealing with the list of transactions, it should be observed that, were a list of both Dr. and Cr. postings, up to this point, abstracted:— (i.) The summations of the two sides would be equal,

(li.) There is a Dr. for every Cr.

(lii.) The *whole* (capital) is equal to the sum of the *parts (i.e.,* the

Drs. less the Crs.)

(e) It will be observed that the Capital Account (Abraham Crosland) is not credited and debited with each item on page 10. As it is usual to prepare a statement of liabilities and assets, the surplus only appears in the Capital Account. That the effect is the same will be seen by comparing the following account with that on page 17.

Dr. Capital Account (abbaham Crosland.) *Cr*

An equipoise, thus established, continues throughout book-keeping by double-entry, so that at any time the correctness of the books may be tested by simply abstracting a list of the Dr. and Cr. postings from the ledger, see Trial Balance, page 2o.

The transactions during the six months are treated as follows:— 1. *Purchased Goods of John Blamires,* £3,2oo.

Dr. Goods Account (ledger folio 2), Cr. John Blamires, (ledger folio 7). Goods Account is the *receiver,* and therefore Dr.; John Blamires is the *giver,* and therefore Cr.

2. *Sold Goods to George Brownson,* £7,2oo.

Dr. George Brownson, as *receiver* (ledger folio 6), and Cr.

Goods Account, as *giver* (ledger folio 2).

3. *Returned Goods (purchased) to Albert Lodge, £75.*

Dr. Albert Lodge, as *receiver* (ledger folio 8), and Cr. Goods

Account, as *giver* (ledger folio 2).

4. *Received Cash, from George Brownson,* £6,74o.

Dr. Cash Account, as *receiver* (ledger folio 4), and Cr. George

Brownson as *giver* (ledger folio 6).

5. *Received from Thomas Allen, acceptance due 1st May,* £2,1oo.

Dr. Bills Receivable Account (/), as *receiver* (ledger folio 1o), and Cr. Thomas Allen, as *giver* (ledger folio 5).

Thomas Allen, in lieu of paying cash, gives a bill (which is an undertaking to pay cash) due 1st May. Bills Receivable are kept in a distinct account under that head

The effect of this transaction is simply that Thomas Allen remains indebted to Abraham Crosland, but instead of the amount of his debt appearing under his own account it is transferred to the Bills Receivable Account.

6. *Paid Albert Lodge, Cash,* £2oo.

Dr. Albert Lodge, as *receiver* (ledger folio 8), and Cr. Cash

Account, as *giver* (ledger folio 4).

7. *Goods (sold) returned from Thomas Allen,* £32o.

Dr. Goods Account, as *receiver* (ledger folio 2), and Cr. Thomas Allen, as *giver* (ledger folio 5).

8. *Purchased Goods of Ephraim Broadbent,* £2,95o.

Dr. Goods Account, as *receiver* (ledger folio 2), and Cr. Ephraim Broadbent (a new account) as *giver* (ledger folio 11), as in No. 1.

9. *Accepted John Blamires' draft, due 17th June,* £4,5oo.

Dr. John Blamires, as *receiver* (ledger folio 7), and Cr. Bills

Payable Account (/), as *giver* (ledger folio 12).

This transaction is the converse of No. 6. Instead of paying John Blamires (/) Bills receivable, *i.e.,* bills for which payment has to be received when they become due.

Bills payable, *i.e.,* bills which have to be paid when they become due.

cash, a bill (which is an undertaking to pay) is given to him, due 17th June. Bills payable are kept in a distinct account under that head. The liability to John Blamires remains the same, but the amount is transferred from his account to the Bills Payable Account. 1o. *Paid ready-money for the purchase of five looms at auction, £179*

Dr. Plant and Machinery Account, as *receiver* (ledger folio 3), and Cr. Cash Account, as *giver* (ledger folio 4).

11. *Received Cash, for Thomas Allen's acceptance, due 1st May, £1,1oo.*

Dr. Cash Account, as *receiver* (ledger folio 4), and Cr. Bills

Receivable Account, as *giver* (ledger folio 1o).

The bill (i.e., the undertaking to pay) having become due, the acceptor,

Thomas AlleD, hands over cash, and the bill is *given* back to him.

12. *Sold Goods to Thomas Allen, ,£"2,8oo.*

Dr. Thomas Allen, as *receiver* (ledger folio 5), and Cr. Goods

Account, as *giver* (ledger folio 2), as in No. 2.

13. *Withdrew Cash from the West Yorkshire Bank, £3,1oo.*

Dr. Cash Account as *receiver* (ledger folio 4), and Cr. the West

Yorkshire Bank, as *giver* (ledger folio 9).

14. *Paid Cash to the West Yorkshire Bank,* 3,32o.

Dr. West Yorkshire Bank, as *receiver* (ledger folio 9), and Cr.

Cash Account as *giver* (ledger folio 4).

15. *Paid Cash in discharge of my acceptance, due 17th June, to John Blamires, ,£4,5oo.*

Dr. Bills Payable Account, as *receiver* (ledger folio 12), and Cr.

Cash Account as *giver* (ledger folio 4).

The bill having become due for payment cash is *given* in discharge, and the bill is *received* back.

The following transactions appertain to Nominal Accounts and differ in character from those already described. Cash is the *giver* in each case, but as no tangible property is *received* in exchange, each class of expenditure is treated as a person (see pages 8 and 9) and is made the *receiver (g).* 16. *Paid Cash for productive Wages, £2,7oo.*

Dr. Wages Account, as *receiver*

(ledger folio 13), and Cr. Cash Account, as *giver* (ledger folio 4).

17. *Paid Cash for Trade Charges, £5oo.*

Dr. Trade Charges Account, as *receiver* (ledger folio 14), and Cr. Cash Account, as *giver* (ledger folio 4).

(g) According to the rule stated on page 7, *every increase or decrease of any part of the property, unless compensated by the like decrease or increase of another part, involves a corresponding increase or decrease of the whole.* Here, *cash* is decreased, but there is no corresponding increase, therefore the property as a whole is decreased. The expenditure after passing into its own special account, and being thence transferred to Dr. of the Trading Account, ultimately reduces the Capital Account, and thus fulfils the rule, (see accounts on pages 20 and 17.) 18. *Paid Cash for Salaries, £24o.*

Dr. Salaries Account, as *receiver* (ledger folio 15), and Cr. Cash Account as *giver* (ledger folio 4).

19. *Paid Dash for Rent and Power, £25o.*

Dr. Rent and Power Account, as *receiver* (ledger folio 16), and Cr. Cash Account, as *giver* (ledger folio 4).

2o. *Paid Cash for personal expenditure, £256.*

Dr. Drawings Account, as *receiver* (ledger folio 17), and Cr. Cash Account, as *giver* (ledger folio 4).

The ledger postings up to this point are given in Roman type, on pages 17 to 2o.

Having recorded in the ledger the Capital and Assets and Liabilities at the commencement of the year, and the transactions during the six months' trading, the accuracy of the book-keeping may now be tested.

Every amount which has been posted to one side of the ledger having its equivalent on the other side (but in a different account), it follows that an abstract of all the items posted to the Dr. side should agree in total with an abstract of all the items posted to the Cr. side.

We therefore prepare what is termed a Trial Balance by making a list of all the ledger accounts and placing in two columns alongside the title of each account:— (i.) The sum of the items posted to the Dr. (ii.) The sum of the items posted to the Cr. See Trial Balance on page 2o.

When the grand totals on both sides of the trial balance agree the one with the other, the book-keeping may be regarded as correct. A further test may, however, be applied by comparing the *total postings,* as abstracted and shown by either side of the trial balance, with the *total entries* from which the postings were made, thus:—

The total postings shown by either side of the trial balance amount to 57. 9Jo.

The entries from which the postings were made are as follows:—

We now proceed to ascertain the profit or loss resulting from the six months' trading.

This may, and should be done by two distinct operations:— (i.) By finding the surplus of assets over liabilities at the end of the six months' trading and comparing the same with the surplus at the commencement.

Thus in our illustration:— £
The surplus at the end of the period is... 4979
The surplus at the beginning of the period is 45oo
Therefore the six months' trading has resulted in an increase of... "479 (A) (ii.) By tracing the precise income and expenditure which has led to such profit or loss.

The former operation may be accomplished with or without the aid of properly kept books, but the latter is essentially the function of double-entry, and its importance is obvious.

According to our remarks on page 8, the accounts given in our illustration should comprise three distinct classes, viz:— (i.) Personal accounts. (ii.) Property accounts. (iii.) Nominal accounts.

Dealing first with the Personal Accounts, viz.:—Nos. 5, 6, 7, 8, 9, 1o («'), 11, and 12 (i), we ascertain from each whether it represents an asset or a liability. The totals of the Dr. and Cr. sides of the accounts Nos. 1o and 12 are equal, and it is only required to rule them off.
£ 58oo

In Account No. 5,

The total of the Dr. side is

Leaving a Dr. balance owing by Thomas Allen of £"338o

This account might be closed, or equalised, by inserting the balance /"338o on the Cr. (or lesser) side, and re-opened by entering the same amount on the Dr. side, thus:— *(h)* To this £479 the drawings £266 may be added, making total earnings £736.

(i) The classification of the Bills Receivable Account and Bills Payable Account is debatable, but they are here regarded as collective personal accounts. It is, however, often inconvenient in practice, and especially so in a manufacturer's books, to bring down the balances of personal accounts in this manner at the time when the balance sheet is prepared. It is quite sufficient to ascertain the balance by subtracting one side from the other.

A list of Dr. and Cr. balances should be made out in this way, as on page 21.

Secondly, the Property Accounts.

Before closing the Goods Account (No. 2) the value of the stock of goods left on hand must be ascertained. The value is assumed at 398o, and that amount is passed to the Cr. of the Goods Account, and is brought down as a Dr. balance to the account for the ensuing half-year. The Dr. balance of,3,98o is recorded in the list of balances on page 21.

After making this entry the postings on the £
Cr. side amount to......... 14o55
And the postings on the Dr. side amount to 963o

Leaving a balance of £a25

The account is closed, or equalised, by transferring *(j)* this balance to the Cr. of the Trading Account (ledger folio 18) as gross earnings, or income for the half-year *(k).*

The Plant And Machinery (ledger folio 3) is assumed to be of the full value (/) shown by the account. The balance is, therefore, merely brought down, and is added to the list of balances on page

21.

The balance of the Cash Account (ledger folio 4), after being compared and verified with the money in the cashbox is brought down in like manner, and added to the list of balances on page 21.

Thirdly, the Nominal Accounts.

The balances of ledger folios 13, 14, 15, and 16 are respectively transferred to the Dr. of the Trading Account as expenditure for the half-year.

The balance of ledger folio 17 is transferred to the Dr. of the Capital Account as money drawn out in reduction of Capital.

Turning now to the Trading Account (ledger folio 18) we find on the Cr. side the gross earnings or income, and on the Dr. side the various items of expenditure of the business. The balance, or surplus, of £735, is the excess of earnings or income over and above the expenditure, and the amount is therefore transferred to the Cr. of the Capital Account as profit.

(j) In transferring an amount from one account to another the entries are always on opposite sides; thus, £4,426 is entered on the Dr. side of the Goods Account and on the Cr. side of the Trading Account. The rule, that every Dr. must have its corresponding Cr., is thus maintained. (i) The balance represents the difference between the cost of the raw goods purchased and the amount realised from the finished goods sold. (I) Tne question of depreciation is treated fully hereafter.

The Capital Account (ledger folio 1) then shows a surplus on the Cr. side of £4979, which is brought down as a Cr. balance, and is recorded in the list of balances on page 21.

The list of balances on page 21 shows exactly the state of every account in the ledger, and from it the Balance Sheet may be conveniently arranged as shown on page 21.

It may be well here to repeat that this Balance Sheet might have been prepared whether the books were, or were not, kept by doubleentry, and the profit of the period could have been ascertained by comparing its surplus of assets over liabilities (*i.e.*, the Capital), with the surplus shown by the Balance Sheet at the commencement of the six months, see page 1o. The Trading Account, however, which is the product of double-entry, shows the precise income and expenditure from which the *profit* arises.

The Goods Account, and the Trading Account, are given in their simplest form and are capable of considerable modifications as will be seen in succeeding pages of this book.

SPECIMEN ACCOUNTS.
Lllustrating Elementary Principles.

Note.—The figures alongside the postings in the following ledger accounts indicate the number of the respective item in the iist of transactions on page 10.

LIST OF BALANCES at the end of the six months'

The specimen transactions employed in the foregoing illustrations are all set out in one list on page io; but there are manifest advantages to be gained by classification before posting the items into the ledger.

For instance there might be a hundred transactions of exactly the same character as No. 2. "Sold goods to George Brownson, £y,200." By keeping these similar items separate and distinct (although it would be necessary to post *each* individual transaction to the Dr. of the respective *customers'* accounts) the aggregate of the hundred transactions might be posted in *one sum* to the Cr. of *Goods Account,* thus saving ninety-nine postings. The same remarks apply to all classes of transactions that are of frequent occurrence.

The importance of this classification was early recognised, and used to be performed every day through the medium of a book called the "Journal." Subsequently, in order to further reduce the number of postings, the journal was written up weekly, monthly, or at other convenient periods, so that the title "Journal" lost its significance. lt will be perceived that the journal is not absolutely necessary, inasmuch as we have posted our transactions to the ledger without its aid, and following the usual fate of things that can be dispensed with it has, to a large extent, fallen out of use or been superseded. The expedient now adopted in lieu of the journal is the use of a *separate book of entry* for each distinct class of transactions. The classification thus goes on as the original entries are made, and the labour of transcribing and arranging the items is consequently avoided. Hence we have the following separate books of entry:—

Sales Day Book.
Purchases Day Book.
Returns Book.
Cash Book.

Each of these books is set apart solely for entering the class of transactions which its title denotes, and the *total sum* of the entries in each book is posted at stated periods.

It is of much importance that these separate books of entry should be properly organised and their rulings well adapted to the requirements of the business. It is one of the chief objects of this work to indicate the books and rulings suitable for Manufacturers.

Although the Journal may be dispensed with it is still of use in some businesses, and it is as well that the exact function of the book should be understood. We therefore give on page 23 a specimen of the most approved form of journal, recording the transactions employed in our previous illustration.

Each of the transactions might be journalised separately, thus:— and so on, but the items are grouped together on page 23 in order to show the method of journal classification.

The foregoing illustrations should sufficiently elucidate the main elementary principles of double-entry; but more or less experience will be required before these principles can be properly utilised in actual practice. Next to experience, skilled guidance in the treatment of details should be sought.

When once the theory is thoroughly mastered, any properly kept set of books may be intelligible from an analytical standpoint, but practice and experience only can efficiently equip the book-keeper for the discharge of his every-day duties.

CHAPTER III.
Manufacturer's Books. Set I.
Simple Transactions.

Having dealt with the elementary principles of book-keeping, the next step is to adapt those principles to the requirements of Manufacturers. In order effectually to accomplish this purpose, it is necessary to resort to practical detailed illustrations. These will consist, in the first place, of a complete set of books in which complicated transactions are avoided, and in the second place, of another complete set of books comprising all ordinary transactions that come within the scope of the legitimate business of a Manufacturer.

The outlines of the system are thus primarily explained by means of a series of simple and uniform transactions that require no departure from the ordinary beaten track. And after the general plan has been made clear, the treatment of unusual, complex, and intricate transactions will, it is hoped, be more readily comprehended.

To avoid a multiplicity of accounts, and to economise space, the imaginary transactions employed in the illustrations are confined to as few names and items as possible, in fact all the details are necessarily condensed. In other respects the accounts furnish an adequate idea of the affairs of a business in actual operation.

The set of books shewn and described in the following pages are supposed to belong to Abraham Crosland, a Manufacturer, residing in Huddersfield. The lists of commencing balances in his Ledgers on January ist, 1884, are given on pages 26 & 27, and are arranged in the form of a Balance Sheet on the same pages.

It is assumed that on January 1st a new set of books is opened, and the balances are transferred into the new ledgers. The folios of the new ledgers, and the supposed folios of the old ledgers, are given alongside the balances on pages 26 and 27.

The method of opening the several accounts in the ledgers has already been explained on page 11, but the learner should trace each item to its respective account.

It will be observed that instead of the amount of the Stock on hand being passed to a Goods Account, as in our previous illustration, it is carried to the Dr. of the Trading Account. There are various classes of goods purchased, which are passed first to distinct accounts, and thence transferred to the Trading Account under their respective heads. The goods sold are likewise treated separately.

The transactions of the business for the six months ending June 3oth, 1884, are recorded in the several books of entry.

At the end of that period, Stock is supposed to be taken, and a new Balance Sheet prepared.

(m) This amount represents the estimated discount to be allowed by creditors on accounts owing to them according to the Purchases Ledger. Observe that there is a Cr. as well as a Dr. balance to Discounts Account.

For convenience of reference the description of the several books is placed after the accounts.

The books employed in Set i are as follows, viz:-

Many of the printed headings of the separate books of entry may be omitted in practice.

Sales
Ledger
Folio.
Name and fall particulars of Invoice.
Biggs & Willet, London
6/4 Worsted A 4...
Holland & Co London
Bartrum & Co London
Biggs & Willet London
Holland & Co London
Bartrum & Co London
Williams & Co Liverpool...
Biggs & Willet London
Biggs & Willet London
Arthur & Co Glasgow
Biggs & Willet London
Williams & Co Liverpool...
Holland ft Co London
Biggs & Willet London
Williams Co Liverpool...
Williams & Co Liverpool...
Williams & Co Liverpool...
Biggs & Willet London
Biggs & Willet London
Holland & Co Loudon
Holland A Co London
Berridge Bros Birmingham.
Biggs & Willet London
Arthur & Co Glasgow
Brown & Co Bristol.
Arthur & Co Glasgow *Post total to* Cr. *of Sales Account in the Private Ledger. Folio 17.*
Amount of each item of the Invoice.
Name and full particulars of Invoice.
Biggs 4 Willet London
Williams 4 Co Liverpool...
Williams Co Liverpool...
Berridge Bros Birmingham.
Williams Co Liverpool...
Holland & Co London
Bartrum 4 Co London
Graham, F., 4 Co Leeds
Bartrum 4 Co London
Biggs Willet London
Murrell 4 Barnes Birmingham.
Arthur Co Glasgow
Berridge Bros Birmingham.
Holland & Co London
Bartrum 4 Co London
Biggs 4 Willet London
Murrell Barnes Birmingham.
Bartrum 4 Co London
Arthur & Co Glasgow
Holland & Co London
Williams & Co Liverpool...
Arthur Co Glasgow
Bartrum 4 Co London
Arthur Co Glasgow
Graham, F., Co Leeds
Bartrum 4 Co London
Brown 4 Co Bristol
Holland 4 Co London *Post total to* Ct. 0f *Private Ledger. Fo. 17*
Amount of each item of the Invoice.
(() Each individual entry in this book is posted to the Cr. of its respective account in the Sales Ledger.
(u) The arrangement of the items in the Trading Account is treated fully in Set II. LEDGER.-Continued. TEST JOURNAL. Quarter ending March 31st, 1884.

Total entries from the Purchases Day Book

Returns and Claims (Purchases) Day

Book....
　Sales Day Book
　Returns and Allowances (Sales) Day Book....
Discounts column of Cash Book left-hand side..
Bank ,, ,, ,,
　Cashier ,, ,,
　Discounts ,, ,, right-hand side
　Bank,, ,,,,
　Cashier ,, ,, ,,
　Bills Payable Ledger Cr. side
　Bills Receivable Ledger Dr. side
　Totals Of Entries posted both to Dr. and Cr. of Ledgers.
4261
29
6100
84
66
3966
1066
27
3906
1064
1840
2086
23,480
Quarter ending June 3oth, 1884.
　Total entries from the Purchases Day Book
　,, ,, Returns and Claims (Purchases) Day Book
　,,,, Sales Day Book
　,, ,, Returns and Allowances (Sales) Day Book
　,, ,, Discounts oolumn of Cash Book left-hand side...
　,, 1, Bank ,,,,,,,,...
　,, ,, Cashier,, ,,
　,, ,, Discounts ,, ,, right-hand side.
　,, ,, Bank ,, ,,,,
　,, ,, Cashier ,,,,,,.
　,, ,, Bills Payable Ledger Cr. »ide
　,, ,, Bills Receivable Ledger Dr. side
LIST OF FINAL BALANCES, June 3oth, 1884.
　Sundry Creditors in Purchases Ledger, see Balance
　　Book, page 63
　Sundry Debtors in Sales Ledger, see Balance Book, page 63　6069
　Bills Payable
　Discounts Account
　Cash Account
　Huddersfield Banking Co., Ltd
　Carriage Account
　Rent and Power, Gas and Insurance Account
　Plant and Machinery Account
　Stock on hand per Trading Account
　Capital Account
　Dr.
3106　10427　19726　PURCHASES DAY BOOK.

In this book are recorded all invoices received for things purchased, and also accounts for work done.

Each page of the example is ruled into five vertical divisions, and the use of each is denoted by its printed heading.

The invoices and accounts received are numbered consecutively and are preserved in a book-file or guard book *(a)* in order of date. The Date, Serial number, Name, and Amount of each invoice are entered in the respective columns of the Purchases Day Book (see example, page 29).

When a page is full the money column is added up and the total carried forward to the top of the following page, and so on from page to page until the end of the quarter.

Posting.—The Date, Serial No., and Amount of each entry are *posted* from the Purchases Day Book to the Cr. side of an account bearing the same name in the *Purchases* Ledger, and the folio of the Ledger is inserted in the column of the Purchases Day Book headed "*Purchases Ledger folio.*"

At the end of the first quarter, March 31st, the entries in the example page 29 amount to a total of £4251 13s. *yd.,* all of which have been regularly posted to the Cr. of the Purchases Ledger.

To carry out the principle of *double-entry* explained on page 8 (see also page 21) this total of the entries during the quarter is posted to the Dr. of the *Private* Ledger.

The Dr. and Cr. postings from the Purchases Day Book to the Ledgers are then equal.

Before posting the total to the Dr. of the Private Ledger it is necessary to find the precise account or accounts to which it belongs. According to the nature of the contents of each invoice its amount is classified under one of the following heads (A), viz:— (i.) Material and Manufacture.
(ii.) Mill Furnishings and Repairs and Renewals to Machinery. (iii.) New Plant and Machinery. (iv.) Incidental Expenses.

After the classification is done the total of the entries for the quarter is posted, in several amounts, to the respective accounts in the Private Ledger represented by the heads above mentioned.

At the end of the second quarter, June 3oth, the entries are classified and the total posted in like manner.

(a) The Guard Book, into which invoices are sometimes pasted, is often ruled with columns and used in lieu of a separate Purchases Day Book. This method, however, is not recommended owing to the cumbrous nature of the book. A separate book for recording the entries and a book-file for preserving the invoices are preferred by the author. *(b)* This classification may be extended indefinitely according to the variety of purchases. In Set II., extra columns are provided for the classification. RETURNS AND CLAIMS (Purchases) DAY BOOK.

Goods purchased are occasionally returned and claims are made in respect of short weight, inferior quality and other matters. Frequent claims are also made upon Outworkers, such as Dyers and Finishers and others, for damage to goods by reason of imperfect workmanship. All such Returns and Claims are first noted on the invoice to which they relate *(c)*. They are afterwards entered in a separate book (rf), labelled Returns and Claims (Purchases) Day Book (see page 3o), which is in the same form, and is kept on the same principle as the Purchases Day Book; the postings to the Ledger being of course *reversed.*

Posting.—Each individual entry is posted to the Dr. side of its respective account in the *Purchases* Ledger, and at the end of the quarter the total is classified and posted to the Cr. of the respective nominal accounts in the *Private* Ledger.

SALES DAY BOOK.

In this book are recorded the particulars of goods sold.

Each page of the example is ruled into five vertical divisions and the use of each is denoted by its printed heading.

The first two invoices in the example, page 31, are entered in full, and represent piece goods, shewing the piece Nos., yards, total yards and prices in distinct columns. The succeeding invoices are set out in total only, as it would be impracticable within the limits of this work to give details.

The ruling of this book may be modified to suit the requirements of the business, but should be so arranged as to show the following essential particulars, viz., (i.) The Date (ii.i The Ledger folio (iii.) The name of the party to whom the goods are sold and the description of the goods (iv.) The quantity, weight, or measure (v.) The price (vi.) The money value of each item of the invoice (vii.) The sum total in money, of each invoice. Additional columns may be inserted for Stock Nos., Package Nos., Marks, Tare, Gross and Net Weights, and any special particulars.

Each entry should be an exact copy of the invoice sent out to the customer. It should be separated from that which follows by a red line drawn across the page as far as the first money column.

The month and the year are written in bold characters at the top of each page.

(c) The person to whom goods are returned, or upon whom a claim is made, should be promptly informed thereof and requested to forward a credit note, or acknowledgement, which when received should be affixed to the invoice.

(d) It is usually sufficient to appropriate a few pages at the end of the Purchases Day Book for recording Returns and Claims in respect of purchases.

When a page is full the two money columns are added up and the totals carried forward to the top of the following page, and so on to the end of the quarter. The totals of the two columns should be made to correspond. As the first column contains the items in detail, and the second column the sum total of each entry, the accuracy of the addition of every invoice is proved by the agreement in totals of the two columns. This is an important check against mistakes in casting up invoices, which are of frequent occurence.

Posting.—The Date, number of page of the Sales Day Book, and Amount of each individual invoice is posted to the Dr. side of an account in the *Sales* Ledger bearing the name of the party to whom the goods are sold, and the folio of the Ledger is inserted in the column of the *Sales* Day Book headed *Ledger Folio.*

At the end of the first quarter *(e)*, March 31st, the entries in the example, page 31, amount to a total of £5,1oo 13s. 8d., all of which have been regularly posted to the Dr. of the Sales Ledger. The total 5,1oo 13s. 8d. is then posted to the Cr. of the Sales Account in the *Private* Ledger.

This done, the Dr. and Cr. postings from the Sales Day Book to the Ledgers are of course equal.

At the end of the second quarter, June 3oth, the sum total of the entries in the Sales Day Book is posted to the Cr. of the Sales Account in like manner.

RETURNS AND ALLOWANCES (Sales) DAY BOOK.

Goods sold are occasionally returned, and allowances are made for returns of packing material, also for shorts, damages, inferior quality, and other matters. All such Returns and Allowances (/) are recorded in a separate book *(g)*, labelled "Returns and Allowances ales) Day Book" (see page 33), which is in the same form, and is kept on the same principle, as the Sales Day Book; the postings to the Ledger being of course *reversed.*

The first entry in the example is given in full and represents piece good returned; the details are omitted from the remaining entries.

Posting.—Each entry is posted to the Cr. side of its respective account in the *Sales* Ledger.

At the end of the quarter, both money columns being cast up, the total is posted to the Dr. side of the Sales Account in the *Private* Ledger.

(c) It is preferred by some to post the totals of the Sales Day Book to the Sales Account every month, and there is no objection to so doing. (/) The Credit Note received from the customer should be preserved for reference. In some houses the credit notes are pasted into a Guard Book, which is ruled with a cash column for extending the amounts. This guard book is made to serve in place of the Returns, &c, book, the amounts being posted therefrom to the Ledger. This method is regarded as inconvenient by the anthor and he recommends the use of a book-file for preserving the credit notes and a separate book for recording them. *(g)* In a small business it is usually sufficient to appropriate a few pages at the end of the Sales Day Book for recording Returns and Allowances in respect of Sales. CASH BOOK.

The labour of the book-keeper may be greatly economised by adapting the ruling of the Cash Book to the special requirements of the business in which it is employed; hence the variety of forms in common use. For manufacturers, whose cash and bank accounts are both under the supervision of one person, the form adopted in the example on pages 34—37 is the most suitable.

Each left-hand page is ruled into six divisions, viz:— Column (i.) For the date.

,, (ii.) For the name, or other particulars of the amount *received.* ,, (iii.) For the folio of the Ledger to which each entry is posted. ,, (iv.) A money column for discounts allowed to parties from whom moneys are received. ,, (v.) A money column in which are entered those amounts that are banked when received. For example, a cheque for £1462 10b. 0d. is received on Jan. 4th from Biggs & Willet, and it is forthwith *banked (i.e.,* deposited with the bank for collection): the amount is entered in the Bank column.

,, (vi.) A money column in which are entered all amounts that, when received, are retained by the cashier to be applied in defraying current expenses *(e.g.* wages and incidentals) or otherwise. Amounts withdrawn from the bank by the cashier for this purpose are likewise entered in this column.

Each right-hand page is ruled into seven divisions, viz:—

Column (i.) For the date.

,, (ii.) For the serial number of the voucher for the payment, which is pasted in the Receipts' Guard Book. ,, (iii.) For the name, or other particulars of the amount *paid*. ,, (iv.) For the folio of the Ledger to which each entry is posted. ,, (v.) A money column for discounts allowed by parties to whom payments are made. ,, (vi.) A money column in which are entered all payments by cheque or order on the bank. Amounts paid by the bank to the cashier for current expenditure are likewise entered in this column, as also the amounts paid by the bank in discharge of Bills. ,, (vii.) A money column in which are entered all amounts paid by the cashier out of cash in his hands.

Generally it may be said:—

All amounts received by the Bank, or by the Cashier, are entered in their respective columns on the left hand side.

All amounts paid by the Bank, or by the Cashier, are entered in their respective columns on the right hand side.

No difficulty should be experienced in comprehending the working of this book after carefully considering each entry of the example in the light of the foregoing explanations as to the uses of the several columns. The only items which it may be desirable to further elucidate are the Cashier and Bank *Coniras*. On January 3oth, for instance, "335 is withdrawn from the Bank *(h)* to be disbursed by the Cashier in wages and other expenses.

In this transaction it is obvious, that:— (i.) The Bank *pays cut* cash 335 (ii.) The Cashier *receives* cash "335

Consequently the amount is entered:— (i.) On the right hand side, in the Bank column, the payment out of the Bank being described as " Cashier, *Contra."* (ii.) On the left hand side, in the Cashier column, the amount received by him being described as " Bank, *Centra."*

This form of Cash Book is in reality a combination of two distinct book, viz: the *Cash* book, and the *Batik* book.

A withdrawal of money, such as above described, requires simply a transfer from the one book to the other, or as we have it in the combined Cash and Bank book, a transfer from the Bank column to the Cashier column ().

(h) It is possible that an occasion might arise when it would be required to pay an amount into the Bank out of an accumulation of cash in hand. In such a case, the contra entry in the Cash book would be simply the reverse of that above described. (i) An objection to the form of Cash book adopted in the example may be suggested because of the apparent frequency of these " Cashier and Bank *contra*" eutrirs, but in an ordinary manufacturing concern this item only occurs once every week or fortnight, and the seeming frequency arises from the necessary condensation of the other entries. Indeed, the compulsory limitation of the number of items in a work of this character renders it very difficult to set forth an adequate conception of a Cash book in actual practice. For instance, on the left hand side (see page 34) we have only one item as received in the month of January from accounts owing, viz:— *biggs at WiUet*, £1462 10s. 0d. *and Discount,* £37 15s. 9d., whereas, in actual business, this one entry would be represented by many items of smaller sums. These remarks apply equally to the accounts paid that are recorded on the right hand side. The following items also, which are repeated monthly, might occur as often as once a week, viz:— Mill Wages, Warehouse and Office Salaries, Crosland, A., Drawings, Traveller's Salary and Expenses.

When a page is full each of the three money columns (both left and right) are added up, and their totals are carried forward to the top of the following page, and so on to the end of the quarter ("/').

Posting.—The Date, Folio of the Cash Book, and Amount *(k)* of each entry on the *left-hand* side *are posted* to the Cr. side of its respective account in one of the Ledgers (/).

The Date, Folio of the Cash book, and Amount *(k)* of each entry on the *right-hand* side *are posted* to the Dr. side of its respective account in one of the Ledgers (1).

The folio of the Ledger to which each entry is posted is inserted *(m)* in the column of the Cash book (whether left or right) headed *Ledger folio.*

At the end of the first quarter, March 31st, the entries on *left-hand* side of the example page 34 amount to the following totals, viz:— £ s. d. £ s. d.

Discounts column 65 11 6
Bank column 3966 o 5
Cashier column 111o 7 8
Less balance of Cash in hand Jan. 1st. 45 7 8 1o65 o o

Individually, all these entries have been regularly posted to the Cr. side of the Ledgers (see note at foot of the example, page 34), and to carry out the principle of double-entry the totals are posted respectively to the Dr. of the Discounts, Bank, and Cash accounts in the Private Ledger. The Dr. and Cr. postings from the *left-hand* side of the Cash Book to the Ledger are thus equalised.

(j) By means of its several columns this form of Cash book takes the place, and discharges the distinct functions, of six separate books of entry.

The left-hand pages answer the purpose of three Day Books for recording:— (i.) Discounts allowed on amounts received,
(ii.) Amounts received which are *Banked.*
(lii.) Amounts received which are retained by the Cashier.

The right-hand pages likewise serve instead of three Day Books for recording:— (i.) Discounts allowed on amounts paid,
(ii.) Amounts paid out of the Bank,
iiii.) Amounts paid by the Cashier.

(k) The amouut of discount allowed is posted to the Ledger, us well as the amount in the Cash or Bank column.
(() Excepting the Cash and Bank balances on January 1st and April 1st, which are *not* posted. *(m)* The respective Ledger to which each item should be posted is indicated iu the descriptions of the Ledgers.

Again, at the end of the first quarter, March 31st, the entries on the *right-hand* side of the example (page 35) amount to the following totals, viz:— £ s. d. £ s. d. Discounts column......... 27 9 1

Bank do. 4955 16 8
Less balance due to Bank Jan. 1st. 1o5o 1o o 39o5 6 8
Cashier column............ 1o64 12 3
Total... 4997

Individually, all these entries have been posted regularly to the Dr. side of the Ledgers (see note at foot of the example, page 35), and the totals are posted respectively to the Cr. of the Discounts, Bank, and Cash Accounts in the Private Ledger. The Dr. and Cr. postings from the *right-hand* side of the Cash Book to the Ledger are thus equalised.

At the end of the second quarter the totals are posted in exactly the same manner.

Up to this point it should be observed that we have proceeded on precisely similar lines in the explanations of the workings of the several separate books.

We have seen that from the Purchases Day Book, the Returns and Claims (Purchases) Day Book, the Sales Day Book, the Returns and Allowances (Sales) Day Book, and also from the Cash Book all the entries are posted *individually* to the Ledgers from day to day, and the principle of double-entry is carried out by posting the *totals* at the end of the quarter to the reverse side of the Ledger.

It remains now to explain a useful function of the Cash book wherein it essentially differs from the other separate books of entry.

By a simple operation we can at any moment verify:— (i.) The balance of Cash in the hands of the Cashier («).
(ii.) The balance owing to or by the Bank (»).

The balance of cash is ascertained by adding the Cashier columns, on both the left and right hand pages, and subtracting one total from the other, the difference representing the amount of cash in hand, (see example pages 34 and 35).

(n) The Cash balance should be tested at frequent intervals, and daily where the transactions are numerous.

The Bank balance should be tested by comparing it with the Banker's Pass book, say ouce every week.

It frequently happens that certain cheques, entered in the Bank columns of the Cash book, are not presented until some time after the date of issue, and it is necessary to take these into account when comparing the balance appearing in the Cash book with that in the Banker's Pass book.

The cashier should always keep a slip of paper in his Cash box shewing the last adjustment of his Cash book, setting out in detail cash, notes, cheques, Ac, in hand. The unpresented cheques should likewise be recorded to show how the Banker's Pass book has been reconciled with the Bank columns of the Cash book.

The balance at the Bank is likewise ascertained by adding the Bank columns, on both the left and right hand pages, and subtracting one total from the other.

The simplicity of this device for ascertaining the Cash and Bank balances, at any moment, is a special feature of the form of Cash book given in the example. To enable this to be done the balances at the commencement of the period are necessarily inserted in their respective columns, and, in fact, the Cash book is made to serve as a complete Ledger account of bank and cash transactions. Nevertheless, it is needful to bear in mind that this is only an expedient for readily ascertaining the cash and bank balances, and it does not affect the essential character of the Cash book as a *separate book of entry*. The total entries (exclusive of the balances at the commencement), like those of all other separate books, require to be posted quarterly *(o)* as above stated, in order that the Ledgers may be complete in themselves, and the Dr. and Cr. postings thereto equalised.

It is only necessary, as in our example, to rule off the Cash book and bring down the balances at the end of each quarter, as the state of the cash and bank accounts can as readily be ascertained when the totals are carried forward as when the Cash book is continually ruled off and balances brought down. It will be observed later on that the bringing down of balances at intervals in the quarter entails more labor in balancing the books.

There are three books required as auxiliaries to the Cash Book, viz:— 1. WAGES BOOK, in which are recorded the details of wages paid, the totals only being conveyed to the Cash book on each pay day (/).
2. PETTY CASH OR PETTY EXPENSES BOOK in which are recorded sundry small disbursements. The total of this book may be entered in the general Cash Book either monthly or at other convenient periods. j. RECEIPTS BOOK-FILE OR GUARD BOOK. For every payment entered in the Cash Book a voucher should be obtained, and fastened in a book-file or Guard Book and numbered consecutively. The consecutive number is inserted in the column of the Cash book headed *Voucher Serial No.* If an acknowledgement is written on the invoice itself, then the invoice number (with the initial " I " for invoice) is inserted in the voucher column. A separate receipt should, however, be obtained in every case *(q). to)* In using the word *quarterly* it is assumed that the books are balanced quarterly. Were the balancing done every month, the word monthly would be substituted for quarterly.

In subsequent remarks on the Bubject of Wages, the wages books are fullyexplained.

(q) Partners may conveniently vouch their withdrawals by writing their initials in the voucher column against the entries of amounts paid to them. See example A.C. for A. Crosland.

The folio of the Wages Book or Petty Cash Book, on which the total entered in the Cash Book is to be found, is likewise inserted in the Voucher column (see example, W.B.2 and P.C.3, &c., page 35).

While dealing with the subject of vouchers, it may be recommended that acknowledgements for moneys *received* by the firm should be given *only on special printed forms* having counterfoils, and it is well to intimate thereon that no other receipt will be recognised.

In concluding his remarks on this most important book, the author would urge the necessity for exercising care and precision in wording the entries, so that they may be intelligible to others at a future date.

THE LEDGER.

In the list of books employed in the example given on page 28, it will be observed that the Ledger is in four divisions *(r)* and on page 25 it is explained that the various accounts contained in the Balance Sheet of January 1st, 1884, are supposed to be transferred from old Ledgers to new ones (s).

Before proceeding to describe the divisions seriatim it may be well to state certain general characteristics which apply equally to every division of the Ledger.

The Ledgers *(t)* are used for collecting transactions *already entered in the separate books of entry,* and arranging them under appropriate headings so as to exhibit each person's account, and accounts of each division of Property, Capital, Income or Expenditure in a concise form.

The process of transcribing the entries from the separate books into the Ledgers is termed *Posting. The Ledgers are for POSTINGS ONLY* and no *entries* («) are made therein. Every transaction must first be *entered* in one of the separate books of entry and afterwards *posted* to the Ledger. This rule must not be disregarded, however small the item, otherwise the books will not balance.

When a personal account is opened in the Ledger, the person's name (surname preceding) and address are written in bold characters (r) If the concern be small the "Purchases" and "Sales" divisions may be comprised in one book. (a) It is not essential that new Ledgers should be obtained when adapting this system to books already commenced. It is sufficient that the totals on either side (subsequent to the last ruling off) of accounts in the existing Ledgers are distinctly shewn. (t) The plural *Ledgers* is used to signify the several divisions of the Ledger. (u) The following are exceptions to the rule above stated:— (i.) In the case of Bills (see description of Bills Ledger). (ii.) When bringing down the balance of an account, which should be done in red ink. (iii.) In closing the Ledger when preparing the Trading Account. on the headline of the folio selected. Property and Nominal accounts are opened in a similar manner by writing the description on the headline.

At the same time that an account is opened the number of the folio selected should be inserted in the Alphabetical Index to the Ledger; (for description and specimen of Index on the Vowel System, see Appendix).

When it is expected that the transactions appertaining to an account will be numerous it is well to reserve for it two or three folios succeeding the one on which the account is opened.

When a folio is full the entries on both the Dr. and Cr. sides (subsequent to the last ruling off) are added up and the totals carried to the folio on which the account is continued. The number of the new folio is mentioned on both sides of the old folio, and vice versa. The new folio is headed in the same manner as the old, and the new folio number is also entered in the Alphabetical Index.

The practice of opening more than one account on the same folio should be avoided, but it will be readily perceived that the limits of this work will not allow a page to each account. In the examples the spaces allotted are intended to represent distinct folios, and are numbered at the right or left hand top corner of each account, as in the case of an ordinary ledger.

When the Dr. and Cr. sides of an account up to a certain date are equalised *(e.g.* when an amount has been received or paid in settlement of a statement rendered) the account is ruled off (see examples) *(v).* THE PURCHASES LEDGER.

Each folio of the Purchases Ledger is ruled into eight divisions. (see example page 38).

Dr. Cr.
side. side.

Columns 1 and 5. For the date of each posting.

„ 2 „ 6. For a brief description of each posting.

„ 3 „ 7. For the folio of the separate book where the original entry is to be found, or the serial number of the invoice.

„ 4 „ 8 A money column for the amount of each posting.

The Purchases Ledger is used in contradistinction to the *Sales* Ledger and its folios are appropriated exclusively for *personal* accounts with firms from whom goods or other requisites are procured, usually on credit.

Hence the *ordinary* postings on the Cr. side of accounts in the Purchases Ledger are all transcribed from the Purchases Day Book, (see Purchases Day Book, page 29, and see also page 57). The ordinary postings on the Dr. side of accounts in the Purchases Ledger (r) In order that the account may be neatly ruled off a line should be left between the postings of transactions payable at different dates.

represent payments, returns and deductions discharging the liabilities incurred for things purchased, and are transcribed from the three following sources, viz.:— (i.) The right hand side of the Cash Book (compare page 62); both amounts paid and discount allowed. (ii.) The Returns and Claims (Purchases) Day Book (compare page 58). (iii.) The Bills Payable Ledger (compare page 69).

In Set II. instances will be given of exceptional transactions causing deviations from the above sources of posting.

The directions given below illustrate the use of the Purchases Ledger, and shew the facility of reference and ease in obtaining information afforded thereby.

ASCERTAIN THE FOLLOW-
ING PARTICULARS, viz:—

1. The date and amount of the last payment to E. & R. Bradley and the discount then allowed.

Also the voucher for the payment.

2. Full details of the goods in respect of which the payment was made. 3. Details of goods returned to them. 4. The amount owing to them on June 30th, 1884. DIRECTIONS. 1. By reference to the Alphabetical Index to the Purchases Ledger we find the folio containing E.& R.Bradley's account is 2. From the Dr. side of their account we ascertain the date of the last payment, June 18, 1884, the folio of the entry in the Cash Book is 2, the amount £824 2s. lid. and the dis-

count £21 2s. 7d. Turning to folio 2 of the Cash Book (see page 87) we find on the right hand side the consecutive number of the Voucher that is fastened in the Receipts Book-File or Guard Book indicated by the figures in the *Voucher column* on a line with the entry of the payment, viz.: 30. 2. On the Cr. side of the Ledger account we find the amounts of two invoices in respect of which the payment was made, viz.: £627 8s. 0d. and £321 7s. 6d., and the invoices themselves, containing full details are traced to the Invoice Book-File or Guard Book by help of the reference numbers 27 and 28. These numbers also guide us to the entry in the Purchases Day Book (see page 29). 3. On the Dr. side we find "May 17, To Returns £3 10s. 0d." and the reference number 28 guides us to the invoice on which the particulars are recorded and also to the Returns and Claims (Purchases) Day Book(see page 30). 4. This is ascertained by adding up the amounts on the Cr. side subsequent to the last payment or ruling off.

Where there are any postings on the Dr. side subsequent to the last ruling off, they would of course be deducted from the total of those on the Cr. side.

THE SALES LEDGER.

The Sales Ledger is ruled in exactly the same manner as the Purchases Ledger.

As its name indicates it is appropriated exclusively for personal accounts with firms to whom goods are *sold*, usually on credit.

Hence the ordinary postings to Dr. side of the Sales Ledger are all from the Sales Day Book (compare page 31, and see also page 59). The ordinary postings to the Cr. side of the Sales Ledger represent amounts received, discounts, returns, and deductions in discharge of the debts due to the concern in respect of goods sold, and are transcribed from the three following sources, viz.:— (i.) The left hand side of the Cash book, both amounts received and discounts (compare page 62).
(ii.) The Returns and Allowances (Sales) Day Book (compare Page 59).
(iii.) Bills Receivable Ledger (compare page 7o).

In Set II. instances will be given of exceptional transactions causing deviations from the above sources of posting.

By way of exercise in the use of the Sales Ledger the reader may ascertain the undermentioned particulars. The directions given on page 67 as to the Purchases Ledger, if reversed and applied to the *Sales* instead of the Purchases Day Book, should be sufficient.
(i.) The date and amount of the last cash received from Williams and Co., Liverpool, and the discount then allowed. (ii.) Full details of the goods in respect of which amount was received. (iii.) Details of the goods returned to them. (it.) The amount owing by them on June 30th, 1884. THE BILLS LEDGERS *(w)*.

An important rule, alluded to on page 65, requires that *the Ledger shall be used solely for posting entries already recorded in the separate books.* In dealing with Bills, however, with a view to economise labor, to facilitate reference, and also to avoid mistakes in transcription, it is expedient to depart from this rule, which is otherwise strictly adhered to. A separate book of *entry* for recording Bills is dispensed with, and the particulars are entered straightway into the Bills *Ledger,* which is ruled into several columns so as to afford a complete abstract of each bill.

It will be observed on referring to the examples, page 43, that the sides on which the particulars of bills are recorded require considerably more space than the sides on which the cash is posted. In order to distinguish the two sides the vertical columns for cash should be ruled with faint *blue* lines and those for the particulars of the bills with *red* lines (see example of Set II.)

There are two divisions of the Bills Ledger, both of which may be bound together in one book.
(w) For full information respecting *Bills of Exchange* see Appendix.
I. Bills Payable.

When a bill is given (or accepted) the particulars thereof are straightway recorded in the several columns on the Cr. side of the Bills Payable Ledger. A serial number, corresponding with the number in the Bills Payable Ledger, is marked on the face of each bill.

The Date given, Serial number and Amount are then entered on the Dr. side of the account in the *Purchases* Ledger bearing the name of the party to whom the bill is given, and the folio of the Purchases Ledger account is inserted in the column of the Bills Ledger headed *Purchases Ledger Folio.*

At the end of the quarter a line is drawn across the page beneath the last entry, the column containing the amounts on the Cr. side is cast up and the total is inserted. (See example page 43).

In the example on March 31st, we find, (i.) A total of £184o 9s. 2d. entered on the Cr. side of the Bills Payable Ledger.
(ii.) A total of 184o 9s. 2d. entered on the Dr. side of accounts in the Purchases Ledger; Folios 1 and 5.

We have already stated that these entries, Cr. as well as Dr., are made individually straightway into both the Bills Ledger and Purchases Ledger without first passing through a separate book of entry, to which fact we shall have further occasion to allude when explaining the use of the Test Journal. Nevertheless, it will be observed that the principle of double-entry, requiring a Dr. for every Cr. in the Ledger, is complied with as each entry is made.

When a bill payable matures the bank is usually advised to pay it. The payment is entered on the right hand side of the Cash book, the amount being placed in the Bank column (compare page 6o, and see example pages 35 and 37). The Date, Folio of the Cash book and Amount paid are posted to the Dr. side of the Bills Payable Ledger on the same line as the particulars of the Bill, and the serial number of the Bill is inserted in the column of the Cash book headed *Ledger folio.*

In order to ascertain at any time the total amount of outstanding Bills, subtract the total of the Dr. column from the total of the Cr. column of the Bills Payable Ledger. The outstanding bills are individually identified by the absence of any amount posted to the Dr. side on a line with the particulars.
II. Bills Receivable.

When a Bill is received the particulars thereof are straightway recorded in the several columns on the Dr. side of the Bills Receivable Ledger. A serial number, corresponding with the number in the Bills Receivable Ledger, is marked on the face of each Bill.

The Date received, Serial number and Amount are then entered on the Cr. side of the account in the *Sales* Ledger bearing the name of the party from whom the bill is received, and the folio of the Sales Ledger account is inserted in the column of the Bills Receivable Ledger headed *Sales Ledger folio.*

At the end of the quarter a line is drawn across the page beneath the last entry, the column containing the amounts on the Dr. side is cast up and the total is inserted (see example page 43).

In the example on March 31st we find, (i.) A total of "2o85 13s. od. entered on the Dr. side of the Bills Receivable Ledger.
(ii.) A total of "2o85 13s. od. entered on the Cr. side of accounts in the Sales Ledger; Folios 2 and 7.

As we have already stated these entries, Dr. as well as Cr., are made individually straightway into both the Bills Ledger and Sales Ledger, to which fact we shall have further occasion to allude when explaining the use of the Test Journal. Nevertheless, it will be observed that the Dr. and Cr. entries of the Bills in the *Ledgers* (Bills and Sales) are equal.

When a bill is deposited with the bank for collection the amount is entered as received on the left hand side of the Cash book in the bank column (compare page 6o, and see example, pages 34 and 36. The Date, Folio of the Cash book and the Amount received are posted to the Cr. side of the Bills Receivable Ledger on the same line as the particulars of the Bill, and the serial number is entered in the column of the Cash book headed *Ledger folio.*

In Set 11. the treatment of bills is explained under a variety of circumstances in which they may be employed and disposed of. It is customary however to deposit with the bank for collection all bills received, either immediately before they mature, or at an earlier date, according to the financial needs or arrangements of the firm (see *Finance).* In our example, page 43, it is supposed that Bills Receivable Nos. 1 and 2 are kept in hand until two days before maturity. Nos. 3, 4, 5, 6 and 7 are deposited in the bank before they become due, in order to provide the bank with funds to meet prospective drafts.

The bank charges for discounting bills are usually included with the commission, interest, &c., and entered in the pass book half-yearly. If specified separately the items should be abstracted from the pass book once every month. In either case the amount is entered on the right hand side of the Cash book (Bank column) as a payment. (See example page 37).

In order to agree and check the amount of Bills in hand, substract the total of the Cr. column from the total of the Dr. column of the Bills Receivable Ledger: the individual bills are identified by the absence of any amount posted to the Cr. side on a line with the particulars.

THE PRIVATE LEDGER ().
The Private Ledger contains Property and Nominal Accounts (compare page 8). It is ruled in a similar manner to the Purchases and Sales Ledgers, except that another money column is added on both the Dr. and Cr. sides, and more space being required each folio occupies two pages instead of one. (See pages 44 to 51).

It should be particularly observed that every book except the Private Ledger and the Cash book might be dispensed with had we only ready-money transactions to record. All moneys entered on the left-hand side of the Cash book might be posted direct to the Cr. side of those Nominal accounts in respect of which they were received. Likewise, all moneys entered on the right-hand side of the Cash book might be posted direct to the Dr. side of those Nominal accounts in respect of which they were paid. In fact, this rule is followed in nearly all transactions where no credit is given: *e.g.,* Jones, Thos., for waste (see Cash book, page 34 and Private Ledger page 51, folio 15), Wages (see Cash book, pages 35 and 37, and Private Ledger, page 48, folio 11), also Warehouse and Office Salaries, Incidental Expenses, &c., &c.

Buying and selling on credit, however, create the need for the employment of the Purchases and Returns Day Books and Purchases Ledger on the one hand, and the Sales and Returns Day Books and Sales Ledger on the other hand, for the *sole purpose of keeping personal accounts.*

It appears therefore that, (i.) In ready-money transactions *(y)* the cash is usually posted direct from the Cash book to the *Private* Ledger.

(ii.) ln Credit transactions the cash is usually posted to the personal accounts in the Purchases or Sales Ledger, and, in lieu of the cash, the quarterly totals of the Day Books are posted to the *Private* Ledger accounts. (iii.) All transactions find their way ultimately into the Private Ledger, either directly in individual items from the Cash book as in Ready-money transactions, or indirectly in totals posted from the Day books as in Credit transactions: the Purchases and Sales Day Books and Ledgers acting as auxiliary books for the sole purpose of keeping *personal* accounts. (x) In Set II. The Private Ledger is subdivided to allow the ordinary business accounts to be balanced by the book-keeper without reference to accounts of a private nature. *(y)* It is convenient in some instances to open personal accounts for ready-money transactions as though credit were given, and, conversely, it is sometimes convenient to treat small credit transactions as though they were for Ready-money. The experience of the book-keeper will enable him to judge in what cases it may be expedient to do so.

It is necessary also to observe that *Discounts* are entered in the Cash book when required for posting to *personal accounts only.* The actual amounts received or paid, *exclusive of discount,* are recorded in those transactions which are posted direct from the Cash book to the Private Ledger.

The ordinary postings to the Dr. side of the accounts in the Private Ledger are from the following sources, viz: (i.) The right-hand side of the Cash book (compare page 62) viz: those entries which represent *ready-money* payments in respect of which personal accounts are *not* opened. Also Cashier, *contra* entries.

(ii.) The quarterly totals of the Purchases Day Book (compare page 57), which represent purchases on *credit* or in respect of which personal accounts *are* opened. (iii.) The quarterly totals of the Returns and Allowances (Sales) Day Book (compare page 59). (iv.) The quarterly totals of the Discounts, Bank and Cash columns on the left-hand side of the Cash book, (compare page 62).

The ordinary postings to the Cr. side of accounts in the Private Ledger are from the following sources, viz: (i.) The left hand side of the Cash book (compare page 62) viz: those entries which represent moneys received in respect of which personal accounts are *not* opened, including Bank *contra* entries.

(ii.) The quarterly totals of the Sales Day Book (compare page 59) which represent sales on *credit,* or in respect of which personal accounts *are* opened. (iii.) The quarterly totals of the Returns and Claims (Purchases) Day Book (compare page 58). (iv.) The quarterly totals of the Discounts, Bank and Cash columns on the right-hand side of the Cash Book (compare page 63).

In the example the current postings for the six months are in Roman type, and the balances, supposed to be brought from the old Ledgers at the commencement of the year, as well as the closing entries, are in italic.

The treatment of the Private Ledger accounts will be further explained in the subsequent observations relating to the preparation of the Balance Sheet and Trading Account.

In Set II. instances of exceptional transactions are given which cause deviations from the above sources of posting.

By way of exercise in the use of the Private Ledger the reader may ascertain the undermentioned particulars, viz:—
DIRECTIONS.

1. By reference to the Alphabetical Index of the Private Ledger find the folio of the account containing the particulars required.

Directed by the reference number in the folio column of the Ledger Account, turn to the page of the Cash Book on which the entry is made, and the consecutive number of the voucher that is fastened in the Receipts BookFile or Guard Book is indicated by the figures in the *Voucher Column* on a line with the entry of the payment. In the case of the Mill Wages, or Petty expenses, the figures in the *Voucher Column* denote supposed pages of the Wages Book, or Petty Expenses Book on which the details are to be found.

2. The alphabetical index gives the folio of the account containing the particulars required and the reference number in the folio column of the Ledger account indicates the page in either the Purchases, Sales, or Returns Day Book on which the details are to be found *(z).* For instance, Material and Manufacture, Jan. 1 to June 30. see Private Ledger, folio 16 (page 60) total £7640 10s. Id. Purchases Day Book folios 1 and 2 (see pages 29 and 30).

It will be observed that many amounts posted direct from the Cash book to the Private Ledger are briefly described in the Private Ledger accounts. In addition to the advantage of shewing at a glance for what each payment has been made, by help of this brief description it can be at once ascertained whether an account has been paid, although no personal account is kept *(e.g.* In Incidental Expenditure account, folio 9, page 48, Jan. 3oth, To Cash, A. & N. audit fee for 1883 £6 6s. od).

The observations in the foregoing pages are commended to the careful study of the reader, who should endeavour to grasp thoroughly the construction and utility of Private Ledger accounts. When once these are fully comprehended, the chief difficulties of book-keeping will have been mastered.
THE BALANCE BOOK.

In the description of the separate books of entry, and of the Ledgers, it has been shewn that when the quarterly (a) totals of the *separate* books are all posted to their respective Private Ledger accounts, *the aggregate of the postings on the* Dr. *side of all the Ledgers is equal to the aggregate of the postings on the* Cr. *side.* (2) As the totals of the separate books are not posted to the Private Ledger until the end of the quarter, particulars required at intervals during the current quarter are obtained from the separate books.

1. The amount paid during a given period for Plant and Machinery, Carriage. Mill Wages, Warehouse, and Office Salaries, Rent and Power, Incidental Expenses, Drawings of A. Crosland, Traveller's Salary and Expenses, *&c, 4c.,*

The voucher for any of the above mentioned payments and the details of Mill Wages and of Incidental Expenses paid through the Petty Expenses book.

2. The amount and details of purchases or *expenditure incurred* during a given period in respect of Material and Manufacture and Mill Furnishings. Also the amount of goods sold and returned.

Therefore an abstract of the quarter's *(a)* postings on the Dr. side of the Ledgers should agree, in total, with an abstract of the quarter's postings on the Cr. side.

The Balance book is designed to receive the details of such abstracts which are prepared to test the accuracy of the Book-keeping and constitute what is termed the Trial Balance (compare page 14).

The book is divided into four sections; the number of pages allotted to each section being regulated by the probable number of accounts to be opened in the respective Ledgers.

The Sections are appropriated as follows, viz:— (i.) For the abstracts from the Purchases Ledger.

(ii.),,,,,, Sales Ledger. (iii.),,,,,, Private and Bills *(b)* Ledgers. (iv.) For a Summary of the totals of the foregoing sections.

Every page is ruled into eleven vertical divisions and Sections i. to iii. are commenced by entering in columns 1, 2, 3, and 4, the particulars (abstracted from the ledgers) indicated by the headings of the columns, viz:—

In columns 1 and 2. The folio and name or heading of every account in the Ledger, entered seriatim on the blue lines *(c)*.

,, 3,, 4. The balance of each account (if any), whether Dr. or Cr., on January 1st, 1884.

In Section iv. a Summary is prepared of the totals of the commencing entries of Sections i., ii., iii. (see example pages 54 and 55).

The Balance Book is then allowed to rest until March 31st, when the first Trial Balance is prepared.

As soon as the quarter's postings are completed the sums of the postings during the quarter on the Dr. and Cr. sides of *each* account are abstracted from the Ledgers and entered in columns 5 and 6 on their respective lines. For instance, (see page 38) Purchases Ledger, Folio 1, Rake, Holling & Co's. account; during the first quarter items amounting to the sum of "1472 1s. 8d. are posted on the Dr. side, and items amounting to the sum of £1og7 18s. 4d. are posted on the Cr. side. These two sums are inserted in columns 5 and 6 of Section i. of the Balance Book (see pages 52 and 53) on a line with the name.

(a) Although in the illustrations the totals of the separate books of entry are posted, and the Trial Balance is prepared, at quarterly intervals, exactly the same lines would be followed in each case were monthly, half-yearly, or other periods adopted. (6) The Bills Ledger is for convenience coupled with the Private Ledger, and is regarded as containing only two accounts, viz, Bills Payable account and Bills Receivable account. (e) When abstracting the particulars from Ledgers that have been in use previously, the heading of every account already opened therein with which it is expected there will be any future dealings should be entered in the Balance Book, although there may be no balance of the account. The headings of new accounts opened during any quarter are entered when the quarterly abstracts are taken out, and follow in order after the accounts previously entered.

The totals of columns 5 and 6 are summarised in Section iv. and if the aggregate totals correspond, the Dr. with the Cr., the accuracy of the postings for the quarter is thereby proved to be correct. Should the aggregate totals not correspond recourse must be had to the Test Journal in order to discover the error which causes the difference.

The Balance Book is again allowed to rest until June 3oth, when another Trial Balance is prepared in exactly the same way as explained above; the quarter's postings from March 31st to June 3oth being entered in columns 7 and 8 *(d)*.

When the Trial Balances are completed, there is in the Balance Book, a compendium of the contents of all the Ledgers, and on June 3oth the balance of every account is ascertained therefrom (compare page 15), in order to prepare a Balance Sheet and Trading Account.

The figures on the horizontal lines of the Balance Book are severally added across the page, and the *lateral total* of each line is inserted in column 9.

It will be observed that all sums abstracted from the Cr. side of the *Purchases* Ledger are entered on the blue or *upper* lines (see Balance Book, Section i., columns 4, 6 and 8, pages 52 and 53) and that all sums abstracted from the Dr. side of the Purchases Ledger are entered on the red or *lower* lines (see columns 3, 5, and 7, pages 52 and 53). In the abstracts from the Sales and Private Ledgers (Sections ii. and iii.) the position of the figures is reversed; the Dr. figures being on the blue or upper lines and the Cr. figures being on the red or lower lines.

This plan is contrived so that all sums on the Dr. side of each account being on a line distinct from those on the Cr. side, lateral additions may be made across the page as on June 3oth, and the respective totals of the Dr. and Cr. sides of each account ascertained. By reversing the position of the figures, as above explained, the *larger* total in nearly every instance comes on the upper line, thus facilitating the process of subtraction. The totals at the foot of each page are likewise carried out on distinct lines.

The totals of the two (blue and red) lines relating to each account are compared and when unequal the smaller amount is subtracted from the larger. When the total of the horizontal line bearing abstracts from the Cr. side of the ledger exceeds the lateral total of the line bearing abstracts from the Dr. side, the difference is entered in column 11 as a Cr. Balance (see Section i., page 53) and *vice versa,* when the total of the Dr. line exceeds the total of the Cr. line, the difference is entered in column 1o as a Dr. Balance (see Section ii., page 53).

(d) Iu Set II. the Balance Book is extended, by the addition of four extra money columns, so as to provide for four quarterly Trial Balances instead of two, and the book might be further extended indefinitely.

The totals of columns 1o and n are summarised in Section iv., and the aggregate totals, Dr. and Cr., if the work is correctly performed, must necessarily correspond *(e)*.

A list of balances abstracted independently from the Ledgers on June 3oth would be identical with columns 1o and 11 of the Balance Book and the balances may thus be individually verified (/).

With the assistance of the list of balances contained in columns 1o and 11, the Balance Sheet and Trading Account are constructed in the manner described in pages 77 to 8o.

Immediately after the preparation of the Balance Sheet each section of the Balance Book should be re-commenced on a new page in readiness for the next half-year's accounts.

At the end of any quarter the amount of the outstanding balance of any particular account, or of the total of the outstanding balances in each of the ledgers, can be readily ascertained by adding laterally the blue and red lines, and subtracting the smaller total from the larger. Thus, to ascertain the total of the Dr. balances in the Sales Ledger on March 31st. See pages 52 and 53.

£ s. d.
Blue or upper line... 6,o54 11 8 + 5,1oo 13 8 = 11,155 5 4 Red or lower line 4. 781 8 8

Outstanding Balances, March 31st... 6,373 16 8 THE TEST JOURNAL.

The Test Journal, which is simply ruled with one money column, is used to facilitate the discovery of errors in the book-keeping at the preparation of the Trial Balance.

The design of the book is based upon the fundamental principle that all the *entries* in the separate books are *posted* (either individually or in total) on both the Dr. and Cr. sides of the Ledgers.

At the end of the quarter, when the Trial Balance is prepared, the totals *(g)* of all the separate books of entry, and also the totals of (c) It has been shewn that the aggregate totals of the alternate Dr. and Cr. columns 3 to 8 correspond one with the other, and the process of subtraction in ascertaining the balances does not affect the equilibrium but merely cancels a like amount on both Dr. and Cr. sides.

(/) In the appendix several methods of balancing are described, and the preparation of a list of Dr. and Cr. Balances abstracted direct from the Ledgers, such as above referred to, appears at first sight to be the shortest possible process. The simplicity of this plan has led to its general adoption, but it affords no clue to the whereabouts of errors in the book-keeping. This defect frequently canses the tedious operation of re-checking all the books in order to discover a mistake.

A recognition of the paramount importance of localising errors, combined with other objects, has cansed many large establishments to prepare detailed analyses of their Ledgers, wherein all the postings are dissected, classified and reconciled respectively with the separate books of entry.

(g) As explained in the note at foot of page t2 the Cash Book, by means of its six columns, answers the purpose of six separate books, and we therefore enter the total of each column in the Test Journal. the Bills *(h)* issued and received during the quarter, are collected and entered in the money column.

On the principle above referred to the aggregate total of this money column should correspond with the aggregate total of the postings on either side of the Ledgers, as abstracted into the Balance Book. For example, the total amount of the entries in all the separate books of entry (including Bills) during the quarter ending March 31st, is "23,48o 8s. tod. (see Test Journal page 56) and the total amount of the postings (whether Dr. or Cr.) as abstracted into columns 5 and 6 ot the Balance Book corresponds with this sum, (see Summary of Balance Book, page 55).

If there should be a discrepancy between the totals of the Dr. and Cr. columns of the Balance Book, by comparing the total of *each* column with the total of the Test Journal it can be at once determined whether the error that causes the discrepancy is on the Dr. or the Cr. side of the Ledgers, or whether there are mistakes on both sides. The correctness of each side of the Ledgers can thus be ascertained separately, and if one side corresponds it is only necessary to examine the other («).

As the particulars required for the Test Journal can be collected and entered in a few minutes, and there may be mistakes of the same amount on both sides of the Ledgers, it is well to have this further proof of the correctness of the book-keeping, even though the Dr. and Cr. columns of the Balance Book may correspond.

THE TRADING ACCOUNT, CAPITAL ACCOUNT AND BALANCE SHEET.

The reader is here recommended to peruse again pages 15 to 17, where the preparation of the Balance Sheet, and Profit and Loss and Capital Accounts in their simplest form, has already been described.

Columns 1o and 11 of the Balance Book (see pages 52 to 55 contain all the balances in the Ledgers on June 3oth. The totals of the balances in the *Purchases* and *Sales* Ledgers, which comprise only *personal* accounts, and also the balances of the Bills Ledgers, are transcribed to a list of final balances, see page 56, prepared on a separate sheet of paper.

It is explained on page 16 that the balances of the nominal accounts which represent expenditure or income are transferred to the Trading Account and the balance of the Trading Account is subsequently (A) It is pointed out in the description of the Bills Ledger, see page 68, that, contrary to all other transactions, Bills are entered directly into the Ledgers without first being entered in a separate book. The total amounts of Bills issued and received during the quarter are, however, eutered in the Test Journal as though they were recorded in separate books.

(i) In Set II. the principle of Test Journal is extended and it is shewn how the Ledgers may be balanced one by one and the Dr. anl Cr. sides of each separately. Mistakes are thus localised and may be discovered by examining only those books where the abstract of entries does *not* agree with the abstract of postings. transferred to the Capital Account. In the specimen accounts (Set I) however, there are certain peculiarities of adjustment which call for further elucidation and it may be well therefore to describe the treatment of the Private Ledger Accounts seriatim.

The closing transfers and entries are printed in italics and should be carefully considered.

The first three accounts in the Balance Book, Section iii., are left open until the other accounts in the Private Ledger have been closed.

Folio 4. Discounts Account (Cr. Balance £1 0s. 4d.)

By referring to the account on pages 44 and 45, it will be seen that amounts are reserved on January 1st to cover discount on the Dr. and Cr. balances at that date. Similar reserves have to be made to cover discount on the Dr. and Cr. balances on June 3oth. The Cr. balances in the Purchases Ledger amount to 2,8o8 16s. 8d., see page 53, and the discounts which will be deducted therefrom, are estimated at £7o 4s. 8d. This sum is therefore entered as a reserve on the Cr. side of the Discounts Account and is brought down to the Dr. side of the same account for the next half-year. The new balance is also transcribed to the list of final (Dr.) balances (see page 56). Conversely the Discount which will be allowed on Dr. balances in the Sales Ledger, is computed at "151 14s. 6d. and that sum is entered as a reserve on the Dr. side of Discounts Account. It is likewise brought down as a Cr. to the same account for the next half-year and transcribed to the list of final (Cr.) balances. When this adjustment has been made, the balance of the old account will represent the true gain or loss resulting from Discounts arising out of the half-year's transactions and it is transferred to the Trading Account.

The proper treatment of the discounts account is of considerable importance and will be further discussed in the explanations of Set II. and subsequently under the head of *Finance*.

Folio 5. Cash Account, Dr. Balance £52 3s. 4d. and

Folio 6. HuddersBeld Banking Company, Cr. Balance £186 19s. id.

The balances of both these accounts are brought down and transcribed to the list of final balances, page 56.

Folio 7. Carriage Account, Dr. Balance £32 15s. 3d. On

June 3oth, £8 4s. 2d. due to the Railway Company is assumed to be outstanding. It is therefore entered on the Dr. side as a reserve. This entry increases the balance to £4o 19s. 5d., which amount is transferred to the Trading Account as the exact cost of carriage for the half-year. The £8 4s. 2d. reserved is brought down to the Cr. of the same account for the next half-year and is transcribed to the list of final Cr. balances, page 56.

Folio 8. Rent and Power, Gas and Insurance Account, Dr. Balance £211 9s. 4d. A reserve is also made in this account for unpaid Rent and Power and Gas calculated to June 3oth, less apportionment of the amount paid in advance for Fire Insurance. This reserve increases the balance to "355 13s. 4d. which sum is transferred to the Trading Account. The 144 4s. od. reserved is brought down to the Cr. of the next half-year and is transcribed to the list of final Cr. balances, page 56.

Folio 9. Incidental Expenditure Account. The Dr. Balance £122 8s. od. is transferred to the Trading Account.

Folio 1o. Contras Account. The Dr. and Cr. sides of this account being equal it is simply ruled off.

Folio 11. Mill Wages Account, Dr. Balance *£1797* 12s. 6d., and

Folio 12. Warehouse and Office Salaries, Dr. Balance £8o 8s. od.

The balances of both these accounts are transferred to the Trading Account.

Folio 13. Drawings Account, A. Crosland. The Dr. balance of this account £16o 17s. od., representing the amount withdrawn from the business during the half-year for personal expenditure, is transferred to the Capital Account.

Folio 14. Traveller's Salary and Expenses Account, Dr. Balance £222 18s. 4d.

Folio 15. Material and Manufacture Account, Dr. Balance £7,614 8s. 9d.

Folio 16. Mill Furnishings, Repairs and Renewals Account, Dr. Balance £237 is. id.

Folio 17. Sales Account, Cr. Balance £1o,791 os. 8d.

The balances of the four preceding accounts are transferred to the Trading Account.

We now turn back to Folio 3, Plant and Machinery Account, Dr. Balance £3225 3s. 7d. This sum represents the value of the plant and machinery according to the balance sheet of January 1st, 1884, with the net cost of new machinery purchased since added thereto. The Wear and Tear during the half-year will have caused a depreciation *(j)* in value, and to provide for this the sum of "118 14s. 6d. (equivalent to per annum or 3f/ for the half-year upon the valuation of January 1st) is entered on the Cr. side of the Plant and Machinery Account and also on the Dr. side of the Trading Account. The balance of the Plant and Machinery Account is then brought down and transcribed to the list of final balances on page 56.

In the Trading Account we have now presented to us an epitome of the expenditure and income arising out of the trading during the half-year.

An important charge, which should never be omitted in calculating the profit of a business is interest upon the Capital employed therein *(k)*. *(j)* The question of Depreciation, one of much importance in the adjustment of the Trading Account of a manufacturing concern is fully discussed in Chapter VI.

(k) If the Capital were borrowed the business would have to pay interest thereon and the proprietor of the concern could obtain interest on his capital if it were employed elsewhere; consequently the concern should be charged with interest as an expense of the business.

Interest computed at the rate of 5 per annum upon the balance of the Capital Account on January 1st, amounts to "365 os. *7d.,* which sum is entered to the Dr. of the Trading Account and to the Cr. of the Capital Account.

The value of the Stock on hand on June 3oth, has now to be entered on the Cr. side of the Trading Account and brought down as a Dr. balance to the same account for the next half-year. It is also transcribed to the list of final Dr. balances, page 56. With the addition of the stock, the Trading Account now shews a surplus of income over expenditure, or a profit gained during the half-year of *£46o* 7s. 3d. The account is therefore closed by transferring that sum to the Cr. of the Capital Account. The balance of the Capital Account is brought down and transcribed to the list of final (Cr.) balances, see page 56.

The list of final balances is then arranged in the form of a Balance Sheet as set out on pages 5o and 51. An explanation of the increase of Capital may with advantage be given in a side note on the face of the Balance Sheet, as shewn in the example.

When the Balance Sheet has been completed, the Balance book should be re-opened by entering therein the Balances in the Ledger as specified in the list of final balances on page 56.

Should any reader desire to accustom himself to some extent to the work of a book-keeper before applying his knowledge in actual business experience, he is advised to write out in foolscap books, ruled as required, the models given on pages 26 to 56. The working of the various books should be followed as though he were engaged in actual business. The items on January 1st, for instance, should be entered in the Purchases Day Book, Sales Day Book and Cash Book and then posted to the Ledger. The items on January 2nd, should then be dealt with in the same way, and so on with each succeeding day. After the entries for a month or two months have been posted, they should be examined so as to ascertain that the postings are correct. When all the entries and postings are made, the books should be closed and the Balance Sheet and Trading Account prepared without reference to the model, which should be consulted only in case of need.

CHAPTER IV.

Manufacturers' Books. Set II.

For convenience of reference the examples of the several books of Set II. precede the explanations.

With two exceptions, the list of books comprised in Set II. is identical with that of Set I.

The exceptions are:— (i.) The Private Ledger, which is subdivided into Nominal Ledger and Private Ledger. The Nominal Ledger receives all nominal accounts that are *not* of a private nature. The Balance Sheet, Trading Account, Capital Accounts and the principal Property Accounts are kept in the Private Ledger.

The result of the trading, the partners' respective interests in the concern and the valuations of the assets are thus kept secret, without in anywise interfering with the progress of the book-keeping or the periodical balancing.

(ii.) An additional book is employed, entitled Mill Sales Day Book, in which are recorded the sundry sales of waste and disused articles, as well as work done on commission. THE PURCHASES DAY BOOK, THE RETURNS and CLAIMS (Purchases) DAY BOOK, and THE MILL SALES DAY BOOK,

follow on pages 82 to 96.

Set II.—Continued.

If the sundry Cuh Sales include articles of radons classes the amount of each olass should be specified in the inner oolumn so that they may be readily analysed. THE SALES DAY BOOK,

and

THE RETURNS & ALLOWANCES (Sales) DAY BOOK, pages 98 to 1o4.

Dobson, Saville A Go
  Atkinson, Blake f t Co London
  Wilson, Henry, ft Co Liverpool
  Dyson ft Rhodes ISJ per cent. June 1st) Newcastle
  Richardson ft Clark London
  Cramer ft Hart Dnblin
  Stocks ft Bolt Birmingham..
  Bnrdon ft Jonea Glasgew
  Starkey, Edgar
  Oannt, Jamea, ft Son Manchester....
  Wilson, Henry, ft Co Liverpool
  Richardson ft Clark London
  Atkinson, Blake ft Co London
cOlefax ft Denham Leeds
  Dobson, 6aville f t Co Bradford
  Dyaou ft Rhodes I8 per cent. June 1st) Newcastle....
  Atkinson, Blake f t Co London
  Burdon ft Jones Glasgow
  Barnett ft Son Birmingham..
  Do. Birmingham..
  Do. Birmingham..
  Brownrigg, Henry Melbourne....
  Cr. Nominal Lsdokr, Fouo 9 3wti«, 1884.
  Dobson, Saville ft Go Bradford
  Wilson, Henry, ft Go Liverpool
  Barnett ft Son Birmingham
  Dyson f t Rhodes I8$ percent. Ang. 1st) Newcastle
  Brownrigg, Henry Melbourne..
  Richardson f t Clark London
  Bnrdon f t Jonea Glasgow
  Richardson f t Clark London
  Dyson 4 Rhodes I3 per cent. Aug. 1st) Newcastle
  Bragg, J. B., f t Co New York
  Cramer f t Hart Dnblin
  Brownrigg, Henry Melbourne..
  Walker, 8terry ft Lark Bristol
  Atkinson, Blake ft Co. London
  Burdon ft Jones Glasgew
  Colefax ft Denham
  Atkinson, Blake ft Co
  Dobson, Saville ft Co Bradford
  Stocks ft Bolt Bil
  Cr. Nominal Ledobr, Folio 9 ®c«m6a, 1884.
  Richardson A Clark (as January) London
  Browurigg, Heury Melbourne....
  Dobson, Haville A Co Bradford
  Barnett A Son Birmingham..
  Atkinson, Blake A Co London
  Whittaker, Bottomley A Co London
  Richardson A Clark (as January) London
  Do. (as January) London
  Barnett *A* Son Birmingham..
  Wilson, Heury, A Co Liverpool
  Atkinson, Blake A Co.. Londou
  Walker, sterry A Lark Bristol
  Richardson A Clark (as January) London
  Colofux A Denham Leeds
  Walker, Sterry A Lark Bristol
  Bragg, J. B., A Co New Kork
  Cannt, James. A Son Manchester....
  Dobson, Haville A Co Bradford
  Burdou A Jones Glasgow
  Btarkey, Kdgar
  Colefax A Denham Leeds
  Cr. Nominal Lkdoer, Folio 9 THE CASH BOOK, pages 106 to 137.

THE PURCHASES or MILL LEDGER, pages 130 to 136.

Nov.

THE SALES LEDGER, pages 138 to 144.

I BILLS LEDGERS.

Bills Payable, pages 146 and 147.
Bills Receivable, pages 148 and 149.

THE NOMINAL LEDGER, pages 152 to 169. 159 THE BALANCE BOOK and TEST JOURNAL, 3 pages 172 to 179. THE PRIVATE LEDGER, pages 182 to 189. DEPARTMENTAL ACCOUNTS.

Selling Departments, pages 192 and 193. Manufacturing Departments, pages 194 to 196.

MANUFACTURERS' BOOKS. SET II.

The books comprised in Set II. are supposed to record the accounts of a firm of Manufacturers carrying on all processes for the production of woollen and worsted cloth. The firm trades under the style of Samuel Blackburn & Co., and consists of two partners, viz., Benjamin Summers and William Blackburn, who are entitled respectively to two-thirds and one-third of the profits, after charging 5 per cent, interest upon Capital. The firm's Balance Sheet on Jan. 1st, 1884, is given on pages 188-9 ('' on folio 11 of the Private Ledger). The Dr. and Cr. Balances of the several Ledgers at this date will be found in columns 3 and 4 of the Balance Book, pages 172,

174, and 176; the Summary on page 176 shewing the totals of each Ledger, which agree with the figures of the Balance Sheet. The firm's transactions for the year 1884 are recorded in the several books; a Trial Balance is made at the end of each quarter; and on Dec. 31st, 1884, Stock is supposed to be taken, and a new Balance Sheet prepared, together with a Trading Account. *As in Set I.*, it is necessary to assume that a new set of books is opened on Jan. 1st, 1884, the balances being transferred from the old into the new Ledgers.

The accounts in this set of books are probably carried out in greater detail, and are of a more exhaustive character, than any yet published; the object being to present as near as possible *fac similes* of books in actual operation, recording a full year's trading, and shewing the whole system from the Balance Sheet at the commencement of the year to that at the close. Without employing a large number of transactions it would be impossible to accomplish this purpose satisfactorily. The terms of payment and the various peculiarities of the trade are illustrated as far as practicable, and every important feature of manufacturing accounts is sought to be comprised in the examples. Where thought desirable, the ruling of the first folio of the book is given in colours in imitation of actual books. THE PURCHASES DAY BOOK.

See Example, pages 82—93.

The method of working this book is identical with that of Set l. (see page 57), except that columns *(a)* are provided for classifying the entries according to the nature of the invoices.

The headings of these columns, together with the subsequent comments on the Nominal Ledger and Trading Account, sufficiently explain their respective uses.

The additions of the columns may be verified by comparing the total of the column headed "Total amount of Invoice" with the aggregate of the classification columns.

It is in some cases convenient to arrange the invoices at the end of each month under the names of the parties from whom they are received, instead of entering them in precise order of date. By way of illustration, the invoices for the month of February are so arranged in the Purchases Day Book, page 82.

An additional column may be provided for extending the total amount of invoices received from each firm during the month, and such total only need be posted to the Ledger account.

Where the invoices received from a firm are many in number, but small in amount, both time and space may be saved by entering the monthly statement in the Purchases Day Book instead of each individual invoice. The invoices may be fastened in the Book-File without serial numbers, and should be marked so as to identify them with the statement to which they relate *(b)*.

Quarterly and other periodical accounts are treated as invoices.

All invoices, delivery notes, weight notes, and other similar documents must be carefully preserved until the statement, account, or invoice to which they relate has been checked and verified therewith, and no entry should be made in the Purchases Day Book without such verification.

An invoice should be obtained in every case where it is reasonable to require one. An Auditor will reject invoices made out by bookkeepers in the employ of the firm, and will require the production of *bona fide* invoices.
THE RETURNS AND CLAIMS (Purchases) DAY BOOK.
See Example, pages 94-5.

This book, like that of Set l. (see page 58), is simply the reverse of the Purchases Day Book, and is provided with columns for classifying the entries.
(a) The ruling of this book may be varied indefinitely, according to the requirements of the business in which it is employed. *(b)* The most convenient method of dealing with many details such as those above referred to may be decided by the Book-keeper according to circumstances, so long as the main principles of the book are observed. THE MILL SALES DAY BOOK.
See Example, page 96.

In every large manufacturing concern a variety of articles are sold representing surplusage and waste *(e.g.* Shoddy, Noils, Flocks, Waste, Seak, &c.), as well as old and disused implements and machinery. Such sales virtually reduce the outlay in the articles from which they arise *(c)*.

Work is in many cases done in various departments on commission, such as Scribbling, Spinning, Dyeing, &c.

The record of both sales and work of the character indicated should be kept entirely distinct from the ordinary sales of manufactured goods, and for this purpose it is convenient to keep a Mill Sales Day Book, all entries in which are posted to the Dr. of personal accounts opened in the Purchases or Mill Ledger *(d)*.

The entries are classified at the end of each quarter, and posted to the Cr. of the Nominal accounts to which they belong.

In extensive manufacturing concerns, especially in those which do not consume their waste products, carelessness in the supervision of the sundry sales at the mill is a frequent cause of dishonesty on the part of those whose duty it is to dispose of the articles. This duty should be confined to as few hands as possible, and the party who sells the goods should not be allowed to receive payment for them. In fact, all monetary transactions, without exception, should pass through the counting-house. Each person entrusted with the sale or delivery of the articles sold should be provided with a carbon paper duplicate invoice book, numbered consecutively; he should be required to make out and hand an invoice to the buyer, and payment should be made to the cashier. Some person, other than the cashier, *(e.g.,* the Auditor) should ascertain periodically that all sales recorded on the duplicate invoices are duly brought to account in the countinghouse. Articles paid for at the time of purchase may be summarised quarterly from the duplicate invoice book, and passed through the Mill Sales Day Book to the Ledger in one total as Sundry Sales. The cash received in the meantime may be entered in the Mill Petty Cash Book, and likewise carried in one total to the Cash Book at the end of the quarter, and thence posted to the Ledger. An illustration of an entry of Sundry Sales (5o 1os. 6d.), and of the cash received in respect thereof, is given in the quarter ending Dec. 31st (see Mill Sales Day Book, page 96, and Cash Book, page 126). Both entries are posted to the Sundry Persons Account in the Purchases or Mill Ledger, folio 23, page 136.

(c) When the Mill Sales are few in number they may be conveniently treated in the same manner as Beturns, and passed through the Returns and Claims (Purchases) Day Book. *(d)* In many instances such sales are made to persons from whom other goods are purchased, and for whom, therefore, a personal account is already opened in the Purchases Ledger. (See Dyson, Mills & Co., page 130 Purchases Ledger, folio 2,) The Sales Ledger is appropriated solely to ordinary accounts with customers to whom only the manufactured artiole is sold, and, for several reasons, no accounts relating to purely Mill transactions should be opened therein. THE SALES DAY BOOK.

See Example, pages 98—1o2.

This book is identical with that of Set I. (see page 58); the details of the invoices are necessarily omitted.

Pattern Day Book.—Where many patterns are supplied to customers it is convenient to keep a separate Pattern Day Book. The particulars of each delivery should be regularly entered therein, but as patterns are usually paid for altogether at the end of the season, the entries should then be classified, and the total only of the deliveries to each customer need be posted to the Ledger (see summary at the end of the March and September entries in the Sales Day Book, pages 99 and 1o1). The several dates and amounts may be set out in the classification, and also on the statement rendered to the customer, but these details may be omitted from the Ledger. This plan avoids the inconvenience of bringing down balances in the Ledger accounts in respect of patterns not due for payment.

The greatest care should be exercised in preparing invoices for goods sold, as balancing the books does not bring to light errors in the computation of quantities and prices. A rule should be firmly established in every counting-house that the calculations made by the person who prepares the invoice shall be checked and initialed by another person, who, for greater security, may reckon double the quantities and half the prices, or *vice-versa.* THE RETURNS AND ALLOWANCES (Sales) DAY BOOK.

See Example, pages 1o3-4.

This book is the same in principle as that of Set I. (see page 59), but it is ruled with three classification columns:— (i.) For goods returned; (ii.) For canvas returned; (iii.) For shorts, damages, and allowances.

The monthly totals of all the columns are summarised at the date when the Balance Sheet is prepared (see page 1o4). The particulars afforded by this summary should be compared year by year, according to the proportions which they severally bear to the total sales. Any excess will thus be brought to notice, and should be the subject of strict enquiry. Where the goods returned exceed the average, the cause usually arises either from faulty manufacture or irregular deliveries.

As in the case of the Sales Day Book, details of the entries are necessarily omitted from the example.
THE CASH BOOK.

See Example, pages 1o6—127.

The principle of this book is similar to that of Set I. (see page 6o), the mode of entering both Cash and Bank transactions being exactly the same.

There are, however, additional columns, the use of which requires explanation. The column on the left-hand side headed "Allowances " is very useful for entering small claims made by customers on remitting their accounts. A manufacturer needs not to be reminded how seldom he receives a remittance without a deduction of something in addition to the ordinary discount. This column saves a separate entry of such allowances in the Returns and Allowances (Sales) Day Book. The practice of including the allowance with the discount is objectionable, as, for several reasons, the discount should be stated separately. The columns headed "Totals Posted" are for the purpose of *arranging the entries according to the respective Ledgers to which they are posted,* in order to localise mistakes when preparing the trial balance *(e).* By means of these columns the classification required for the Test Journal is performed instantaneously at the end of the quarter.

In the books of a manufacturer it will be observed, in practice as well as in the examples given, that almost every entry on the left-hand side of the Cash Book is posted either (i.) to the Sales Ledger, or (ii.) to the Nominal or the Bills Ledger. In case of an occasional entry that has to be posted to the *Purchases* Ledger, it should be written in *red ink (/) (e.g.,* April 8th, Mitchell, Jonathan, £*11* 17s. 6d.), and the initial letters P.L. should be placed against the Ledger folio (see page 112). Conversely almost every entry on the right-hand side is posted either (i.) to the Purchases Ledger, or (ii.) to the Nominal or the Bills Ledger. In case of an occasional entry that has to be posted to the *Sales* Ledger, it should be written in *red ink (/) (e.g.,* Jan. 28th, Bragg, & Co., £15 4s. 7d.), and the initial letters S.L. should be placed against the Ledger folio (see page 107) *(g).*

In checking the postings the bookkeeper should call over and compare with the Ledgers the several amounts extended into one classification column before passing to those extended into another column. He will thus effectually guard against amounts being extended into the wrong column.

(c) Very little extra labour is caused by the UBe of these columns, as in posting to the Ledger the cash and discount are necessarily added together, and the addition can nowhere be more conveniently made than alongside the entry. (/) In the example these entries are printed in black type to represent red ink; the latter item is printed in red. *(g)* In certain businesses it is convenient to have three Ledger classification columns on each side of the Cash Book—(i.) For the Sales Ledger, (ii.) For the Purchases

Ledger, (iii.) For the Nominal and Bills Ledgers.

It is obvious that the sum of the totals of the classification columns should agree with the sum of the totals of the columns containing the entries (*i.e.,* the Allowances, Discounts, Cashier, and Bank columns). Of course, the commencing and closing *balances* (Cash and Bank) must be omitted from consideration.

The entries described as " Petty Cash, Warehouse," and "Petty Cash, Mill," represent Cash supposed to be handed to sub-cashiers for small disbursements. The payments made by the sub-cashiers should be recorded in petty cash books to be submitted periodically to the chief cashier for him to inspect and verify. The Petty Cash Books should be used only for very small disbursements, and *no entries must be made therein that require to be posted to the Ledgers.* If desired, a special column may be added to the Cash Book for extending entries of incidental expenses, the total of which may be posted quarterly. The Petty Cash Books may be ruled with columns for classifying the payments, but this is necessary for manufacturers only in comparatively few instances.

THE LEDGERS.

The explanations given in the descriptions of the several Ledgers of Set I. apply equally to those of Set II. It will, therefore, only be necessary to supplement the remarks on pages 65—73 by explaiping the treatment of accounts containing transactions which do not conform exactly to the rules already laid down.

It will be observed that both discount and cash (or bill) are in every instance posted in one sum to the Ledger accounts, the amount of the discount being stated alongside. It is preferred by some to post the discount and cash in separate items, as in Set I. The adoption of either method may be left to the choice of the book-keeper, but the exact amount of discount allowed should always be set out in the Ledger for future reference.

THE PURCHASES or MILL (h) LEDGER.

See Example, pages 13o—136.

In posting to the Cr. side of the Purchases Ledger from the Purchases Day Book, it is convenient to mention the class of goods comprised in the purchase (*e.g.,* " Material," "Dyewares," &c.,), and it will be observed that this is done in the example.

(*h*) The words " or Mill" are added becanse the Purchases Ledger is usually kept at the mill and the Sales Ledger at the warehouse (if any). Moreover the Mill Sales are posted to the Purchases Ledger (see Mill Sales Day Book). It is often convenient for the Sales and Returns Day Books, the Bills Receivable Ledger and the Sales Ledger, together with a separate Cash Book, to be kept at the warehouse and balanced apart from the remaining books, which are kept at the mill. When this is done all payments, except for petty expenses, should be made at the mill, the Warehouse Cash Book being used solely for cash received.

The following accounts require special comment, viz:—

Merton, Walker & Co., London. Folio 7, page 133.

This account shews how to treat a small payment made by the firm for carriage of goods purchased, which is recoverable from the vendor. The payment made on Feb. 17th is entered in the Cash Book (see page 1o9, folio 2) and posted direct to the Dr. of this account. The account also shews how to rectify an overcharge on goods purchased. The amount of the overcharge is entered on March 28th, in the Returns and Claims (Purchases) Day Book (see page 94) and is posted to the Dr. of this account.

Littlewood, Wilson & Co., Batley. Folio 18, page 136.

This account shews how small amounts of *interest* (i) may be posted to personal accounts. A note is inserted in the account stating that the machinery purchased is to be paid for by instalments of £1oo per quarter, with interest at 5 per cent, per annum. It is therefore necessary, as each quarterly payment becomes due, to credit Littlewood, Wilson & Co. with the amount of interest accrued to date. Bearing in mind the rule (see page 65) that the Ledger is for *postings only,* the amount of interest is first *entered* in the Discounts column on the left hand side of the Cash Book (see pages 116, 12o and 126).

Rushforth, R. & Co., Huddersfield. Folio 21, page 136.

The firm is' supposed both to *buy* material from and to *sell* manufactured goods to R. Rushforth & Co.; and an account bearing their name is opened in the Purchases Ledger and another in the Sales Ledger (see page 143, S.L., folio 14). On July 21st a settlement is made of both accounts as follows:— £ s. d.

R. Rushforth & Co. are Creditors for goods purchased from them (see Purchases Ledger, folio 21)... 79 18 11

Less Discount

R. Rushforth & Co. are Debtors for goods sold to them (see Sales Ledger, folio 14) 54 5 1

Less Discount 1 6 1 52 19 o

Leaving a balance due to them of... 23 1o o (t) The manner of dealing interest on loans is referred to on page 216. Items of interest of the character above described are rare in a prosperous business, but where they are at all numerous it may be desirable to appropriate a small book, or portion of a book, in which to record the entries.

These and other abnormal transactions may be journalised, but the use of the Journal iu ordinary oases is undesirable, and it is seldom that it cannot be dispensed with.

A cheque for "23 10s. od. is handed to R. Rushforth & Co. in settlement of both accounts. This transaction is entered as though the amount owing by R. Rushforth & Co. had been received and the full amount owing to them had been paid.

Thus—on the left hand side of the Cash Book, in the Cashier column, £52 19s. od. is entered as received; on the right hand side of the Cash Book, in the Cashier column, "52 19s. od., and in the Bank column, £23 1os. od. are entered as paid (see Cash Book, folio 7, pages 118, 119). The discounts allowed both on the purchases and on the sales account can thus be entered in the ordinary way.

Accounts of this character do not often arise, and it is only desirable to keep a distinct account in the Sales Ledger where the *goods sold* are the manufactured article sold by the firm. As already stated on page 199, accounts relating to Sales at the Mill should be entered in the Mill Sales Day Book and posted to the Purchases *or Mill* Ledger. Both purchases and sales can then be carried to one account; the balance received or pnid in settlement being entered and posted in the ordinary way *(e.g., Jonathan Mitchell, folio 14, page 135).*

Sundry Persons Account. Folio 23, page 136.

This account is for *small purchases* from firms with whom no further transactions are anticipated, and also for *small sales at the mill* (see *Mill Sales Day Booh).* In all cases where the transactions with a firm are likely to be continued a separate Ledger account should be opened in the name of that firm.

THE SALES LEDGER.

See Example, pages 138—144.

The following accounts require explanation, viz:—

Atkinson, Blake & Co., London. Folio 1, page 138.

This account shews the method of dealing with a smal *balance left over* in settling a statement of goods due for payment. The £3 5s. *yd.* carried down in italic (red ink) may represent a parcel of patterns which becomes due for payment at a later date than the current deliveries of goods. A more satisfactory method of dealing with patterns, when numerous, is described on page 2oo. The £3 5s. *yd.* also serves to illustrate the manner in which a disputed claim, or an error in a remittance, may be brought down pending a settlement. Such balances should always be written in red ink in order to distinguish them, and to guard against their being cast up as postings when preparing the trial balance.

Richardson & Clark, London. Folio 2, page 138.

This account shews the method of posting goods in respect of which a *special date is fixed for payment*, differing from the ordinary trade terms of credit. The due date for payment is indicated by the words "as June," "as January."

Bragg, J. B. & Co., New York. Folio 5, page 14o.

This account shews the method of dealing with *charges paid for and on behalf of a customer,* which are reclaimable from him.

The several payments on behalf of J. B. Bragg & Co. are posted from the Cash Book to the Dr. of their account.

Where a fixed rate is added to the sale price to cover freight, duty, insurance, &c., or where such charges are included in the sale price, both goods and charges are comprised in the invoice of the goods and entered in the Sales Day Book. The outlay by the firm should be treated as an additional element of cost of the goods, and should be posted to a distinct Nominal account, being thence transferred to Section I. of the Trading Account.

Wilson, Henry & Co., Liverpool. Folio io, page 142.

This account shews *how to distinguish the items comprised in each settlement,* when it is impracticable to divide them by ruling off the account.

The items marked by the letters a.a., b.b., on one side of the account, respectively balance the items marked by the same letters on the other side.

Burdon & Jones, Glasgow. Folio 11, page 142.

This account illustrates the method of treating *moneys received through an agent, who deducts his commission therefrom.*

The *full amount* received from Burdon & Jones is in each instance entered on the left hand side of the Cash Book, and the amount retained by the agent, John Alexander, is entered, as though it were paid to him, on the right-hand side of the Cash Book. The total of the customer's remittance may either be posted to the Ledger in one item, or the commission may be posted separately, as in the example.

It will be observed that the amount of the commission is entered on each side of the Cash Book in the *Cash* columns, as only the net amount received from the agent actually passes into the bank.

Harrop, Jonas & Sons, Halifax. Folio 12, page 143.

This account shews—

(a) How to deal with a *dishonoured cheque.*

The amount of the dishonoured cheque is entered on the righthand side of the Cash Book in the Bank column, and is posted to the Dr. of Jonas Harrop & Sons, from whom it was received.

(b) How to deal with the account of a customer who *compounds with his creditors.*

Promissory notes for the amount of the composition are supposed to be received, and these are entered on the Dr. side of the Bills Receivable Ledger and also on the Cr. side of,the insolvent customer's account. The balance, representing the net loss after giving credit for the composition received, is transferred to the Bad Debts account in the Nominal Ledger (see page 164). The amount transferred is recorded in the Test Journal (see page 178).

Bentley & Robinson, Stroud. Folio 13, page 143.

This account shows—

(a) How to deal with a *dishonoured bill.*

The bill in this case has been deposited with the bank for collection in the ordinary course. When dishonoured, the amount (both of the bill and expenses of noting, &c., as charged by the bank, viz. , "237 5s. od.), is entered on the righthand side of the Cash Book in the Bank column (see page 119), and is posted to the Dr. side of Bentley and Robinson's account. Any additional expense incurred through the dishonour of the bill *(e.g.,* bank commission not charged by the bank until the end of the halfyear) is entered in the Discounts column of the Cash Book alongside the amount of the bill, and is also posted to the Dr. of the customer's account (see item 5s. 6d.). The Cash Book entry should, unless immediately posted to the Ledger, describe the payment fully; in the example the description is given only in the Ledger.

(b) How to deal with an *insolvent account* where the settlement of the debtor's affairs is likely to be prolonged.

The whole balance due is transferred

straightway to the Bad Debts account. Dividends on account of the debt are posted when received to the Cr. of the Bad Debts account (see page 165).

Rushforth, R. & Co., Huddersfield. Folio 14, page 143.

(See Purchases Ledger, page 2o3).

Watkinson, Joshua, Huddersfield. Folio 15, page 143.

In paying his account Joshua Watkinson is supposed to hand over one of his own *customer's cheques* for more than the amount due, the surplus, £5 1s. 8d. , being returned to him in cash. The cheque received being *banked* by the firm, is entered on the left-hand side of the Cash Book in the Bank column (see page 114) and is posted to the Cr. of Watkinson's account. The surplus paid back to him in cash is entered on the right-hand side of the Cash Book, in the Cash column, and is posted to the Dr. of his account. Were the surplus returned in a cheque, the amount would of course be entered in the right-hand *Bank* column.

Dyson & Rhodes, Newcastle-on-Tyne. Folio 17, page 144.

This account, like folio 2, shows how *special terms,* upon which goods are sometimes sold, should be stated in the Ledger, *e.g.,* "3$ June 1st," indicating that payment is due less 3I per cent, discount on June 1st.

Stocks & Bolt, Birmingham. Folio 18, page 144.

This account illustrates the treatment of a *renewed bill.*

Bill No. 22 is supposed to have been deposited in the bank on the 9th December, the amount being entered in the ordinary course on the left-hand side of the Cash Book on that date (see page 124), and posted to the Cr. of the Bills Receivable Ledger (see page 149). On December 12th Stocks & Bolt request a renewal of the bill for two months, agreeing to pay interest. The bank, being thereupon advised, retires the bill, and the amount is entered on the right-hand side of the Cash Book in the Bank column; the transaction being equivalent to a payment by the bank. The two months' interest *(£2* 17s. iod.) is entered in the Discounts column, and both the amount and interest are posted to the Dr. of Stocks & Bolt's account, as a payment made on their behalf. The renewed bill, which, with interest added, amounts to /"35o 6s. 4d. is entered when received in the ordinary way.

Sundry Persons Account. Folio 2o, page 144.

This account is for small sales to persons for whom it is not worth while to open a special account.

The item on Feb. 4th (Wm. Blackburn, £1 2s. od.) represents a small sale to one of the partners. It is desirable that the partner, as in the example, should pay cash for such transactions, but the amount might be transferred to his Drawings account.

THE BILLS LEDGERS.

Bills Payable. See Example, pages 146-7.

The only variations in this book from that of Set I. are the additional column for entering discount allowed alongside the amount of each bill and the monthly division of the column for the due dates.

When a bill is given in settlement of an account it is usually for the full amount, but odd shillings and pence are frequently written off and must be treated as discount. The ordinary trade discount is sometimes claimed, less the Banker's charge for discounting the bill, and in such cases the difference is treated as the amount of discount allowed.

The amount both of the discount and the bill is entered in one sum to the Dr. of the respective account in the Purchases Ledger.

The total of the Discounts column is posted quarterly to the Cr. of the Discount on Purchases account in the Nominal Ledger (folio 22, page 165).

Bills Receivable. See Example, pages 148-9.

A column is added for discounts, as in the Bills Payable Ledger, and the total of the Discounts column is posted quarterly to the Dr. of the Discount on Sales account in the Nominal Ledger (folio 21, page 162). The due date column is ruled with monthly divisions.

Nos. 6, 7, 8, and 9, received from Jonas Harrop & Sons, represent *Promissory Notes (j)* for the amount of *composition* on their debt.

These notes are treated in the same manner as bills, except that a memorandum is added describing them as promissory notes and giving the name and address of the surety (see page 148).

Nos. 1o and 11 shew the method of treating bills that are *discounted otherwise than through tlie firm's Banker.*

The charge for discounting, £10 18s. yd., is entered in the Discounts column of the Cash Book, folio 3, page 11o, alongside the amount received from the Discount Company, and both the charge for discounting and cash are posted to the Cr. of the Bills Ledger.

No. 12, received from Bentley & Robinson, represents a *customer's bill (i.e.,* a bill accepted by one of Bentley & Robinson's own customers).

The name and address of the acceptor and drawer are recorded, as they would be required were the bill dishonoured. The names and addresses of indorsers, if any, should also be set out; in fact all the material particulars of the bill.

No. 27. This bill is marked as a *renewal (k)* of No. 22.

Nos. 1, 16, 2o, 23, and 28 are drafts on a third party, which would be presented for acceptance of the drawee (see *Bills of Exchange).*

The method of dealing with renewed bills is described on page 2o7.

The treatment of *dishonoured* bills is explained on page 2o6.

Where a Bill Receivable is handed over by the firm to one of its own creditors in discharge of a debt, the amount of the bill is entered on the left-hand side of the Cash Book, as received, and posted to the Cr. of the Bills Ledger. The amount is also entered on the right-hand side of the Cash Book, as paid, and posted to the Dr. of the creditor's account. Payment by customer's bill is seldom resorted to except in case of need, or unless a marked advantage is to be gained thereby. It is regarded amongst home traders as *prima facie* evidence of financial weakness.

Where it is often necessary to record any further material particulars, additional columns may be added *(e.g.,* for the acceptor's and drawer's name and address; for currency; for the details of discount or exchange, &c., &c.).

(j) It is in some cases convenient to appropriate a distinct portion of the Bills Ledger to promissory notes and bills received from insolvents, especially where they are numerous. As these instruments frequently extend over long periods, if entered with the current bills they not only cause difficulties in balancing, but are liable to be overlooked and neglected. (k) It may here be remarked that bills should never be renewed until full enquiry has been made into the circumstances which have caused the customer to request renewal.
THE NOMINAL LEDGER.
See Example, pages 152—169.

This is a sub-division of the Private Ledger appropriated to all those accounts which do not belong either to the Purchases or Sales Ledger.

The Nominal Ledger, strictly should be confined to nominal accounts. It is, however, often convenient to keep therein any personal accounts that do not properly belong either to the Purchases or the Sales Ledger, and also which are not required to be kept entirely secret. All transactions of a private nature are, for the time being, posted without particulars to a *Private Ledger account* (/) (see folio 31, pages 168-9).

The accounts in the Nominal Ledger are referred to *seriatim* in the description of the Trading Account.

The transfers in several of the accounts at the end of the year, also the closing entries and the balances brought down (both *Reserves and Stock*) are entered *after the final trial balance has been prepared in the Balance Book*. THE BALANCE BOOK.
See Example, pages 172—177.

The principle of this book is identical with that of Set I., but it has four additional money columns to provide for the Dr. and Cr. postings of *four* quarters instead of two.

The Dr. and Cr. balances in the *Private* Ledger at the commencement of the year are cast up, and the totals are entered on either side of the Private Ledger account that is kept in the Nominal Ledger (see folio 31, pages 168-9). All the transactions during the year that are posted to the Private Ledger are also posted to this account, consequently the books can be balanced periodically without reference to the Private Ledger.

For convenience, the abstracts from the Bills Ledger are entered under Section iii. of the Balance Book, as though the Bills Payable and Bills Receivable accounts belonged to the Nominal Ledger.

In abstracting the postings from the Ledger Accounts, it is convenient to tick, thus *V,* beneath the last posting in each quarter on both the Dr. and the Cr. side, so as to distinguish them from the postings of the succeeding quarter (see example in Brandram, Reeves & Co.'s account, page 13o).

The method of carrying forward the totals of the several columns of the Balance Book to the top of the succeeding page is shewn in the example. It is better, however, where many pages of the Balance Book are employed, to carry the totals of each page to a summary and not to carry them forward from page to page.

(2) The particulars of the Private Ledger items in the example are given in the Cash Book, but in practice the entries may be so made as not to reveal their nature anywhere but in the Private Ledger. THE TEST JOURNAL.
See Example, pages 178—179.

This book shews an extension of the principle of the Test Journal described on pages 76-7. In addition to the single money column as in Set l. (see page 56), six further columns are provided for classifying the entries *according to the Ledgers to which they have been posted*—three columns for the Dr. side and three for the Cr. side. The columns on either side are respectively headed (i.) The Purchases Ledger, (ii.) The Sales Ledger, and (iii.) The Nominal and Bills Ledgers.

It is stated on page 77 that the grand total of the *entries* abstracted into the Test Journal should agree with the grand totals of the *postings* abstracted into the Balance Book. It follows, therefore, that when the entries are classified in the Test Journal, the total of each *column* of the Test Journal should agree with the total of the corresponding *section* of the Balance Book.

The total of the entries in each of the separate books, except the Cash Book, can be classified instantly. It has already been explained that the entries are posted as follows, viz:—

The entries in the Purchases Day Book are posted to

The entries in the Returns and Claims (Purchases) Day Book are posted to

The entries in the Mill Sales Day Hook are posted to

The entries in the Sales Day Book are posted to

the Cr. of the *Purchases* Ledger in individual items, and to the Dr. of the *Nominal* Ledger in quarterly totals.

the Dr. of the *Purchases* Ledger in individual items, and to the Cr. of the *Nominal* Ledger in quarterly totals. the Dr. of the *Purchases* or Mill

Ledger in individual items, and to the Cr. of the *Nominal* Ledger in quarterly totals.

the Dr. of the *Sales* Ledger in individual items, and to the Cr. of the *Nominal* Ledger in monthly totals. the Cr. of the *Sales* Ledger in individual items, and to the Dr. of the *Nominal* Ledger in monthly totals. the Bills to the Cr. of the *Bills Payable* Ledger individually, and the Discount to the Cr. of the *Nominal* Ledger iu quarterly totals, and to the Dr. of the *Purchases* Ledger individually, both Bills and Discount.

£the Bills to the Dr. of the *Bills Receivable* Ledger individually, and the Discount to the Dr. of the *Nom*The Bills Receivable, including Discount,. *inal* Ledger in quarterly totalB, and are posted to the Cr. of the *Sales* Ledger individually, both Bills and Discount.

The entries in the Returns and Allowances

(Sales) Day Book are posted to

The Bills Payable, including Discount, are J posted

The individual entries in the Cash Book, as explained on page 2o1, are classified as the book-keeping proceeds, and at the end of the quarter a note is made on either side of the Cash Book shewing the total of the entries posted to each Ledger (m) (see pages 11o and 111). From this note the classification is made in the Test Journal.

In case of a *transfer* from one Ledger account to another, as there is no separate book of entry for transfers, the amount is entered separately in the Test Journal (see examples).

In the examples, the quarterly totals of the several classification columns of the Test Journal will be found to correspond in each case with the quarterly totals of the corresponding sections of the Balance book. In the event of a discrepancy arising when the Trial Balance is being prepared, it is only necessary to examine the entries and postings comprised in the particular column and section where the discrepancy appears. Errors being thus localised the Ledgers can be balanced one by one, and the Dr. and Cr. sides of each separately.

It may be useful to point out that, provided the original entries in the separate books have been faithfully recorded, a principal may satisfy himself of the absolute accuracy of the book-keeping by preparing the Test Journal himself, and seeing that it corresponds with the Balance Book, which may be entered up by the book-keeper.

THE TRADING ACCOUNT *(n)*, CAPITAL ACCOUNT AND BALANCE SHEET.

The mode of preparing the Trading Account, Capital Account and Balance Sheet having been fully explained on pages 15—17 and 77—8o, it is only necessary here to consider the treatment of those nominal accounts which contain items of a special nature, or which differ in their final adjustment from the more simple accounts already described. In the Summary of the Balance Book, columns 14 and 15 (see page 177), we have presented to us the total of the balances in each of the Ledgers on December 31st, 1884. The total balances of the Purchases and Sales Ledgers are transcribed straightway to a list of final balances prepared on a separate sheet of paper (see page 184-5). The balances of the Nominal Ledger are, however disposed of individually; those which represent Expenditure or Income being transferred to the Trading Account, and those which represent Liabilities or Assets being transcribed to the list of final balances.

(m) The Cash and Bank balances at the commencement of each quarter are not posted to the Ledger, but appear in the Cash Book merely as memoranda for the purpose of testing at any time during the quarter the state of the Cash and Bank accounts. The amounts of such balances are therefore deducted from the totals to be entered in the Test Journal (see uote in Cash Book, page 110, 111). (n) The Trading Account of a manufacturing concern combines both the Goods Account and the Profit and Loss Account. The term Profit and Loss Account, strictly, describes an account which shews the profit or loss resulting from each of the several enterprises or adventures of the firm. The title Trading Account applies to an account of Income and Expenditure of a trading concern. Where more than one concern is carried on by the same firm, the result of the trading of each may be carried to a Profit and Loss account (see also *Departmental Accounts)*.

In closing the Nominal accounts, attention should be given to the points referred to in the following observations.

In the Trading Account of Set I., for the sake of simplicity, the Stock is set out as a whole, whereas in the Trading Account of Set II. only that part of the stock is set out which comprises Material in process of manufacture and Finished goods (o). The remaining stock is distributed to the following accounts which receive their respective portions, viz:—

Material account, folio I.
Dyewares account, folio 2.
Chemicals, Soap, Size, Oil, &c. account, folio 3.
Packing Material account, folio 5.
Motive Power account, folio 1o.
Mill Furnishings, Repairs, and Renewals to Machinery account, folio 12.
Stables account, folio 13.

The stock is thus distributed in order to arrive at the actual cost of material or articles *consumed* under each of the above heads.

Mill Wages Account. Folio 8, pages 154-5.

All the wages paid at the Mill are regularly posted to this account, and transfers are made when the Trading Account is prepared. The several amounts to be transferred to other accounts are ascertained from the classification in the Wages books (see *Wages)*.

Motive Power Account. Folio 1o, pages 156-7.

This account is not required in Set I. , where both Room and Power are included in the Rent and Power, &c. account, the machinery being turned at the expense of the landlord. Here, however, rent is paid for the mill premises and the firm provides motive power for itself.

All expenditure incurred in driving the machinery and keeping the engine, boilers and gearing (or motive plant) in working order, is charged to this account *(e.g.,* outlay in coal, tallow, lubricating oil, repairs to motive plant, and wages). The total amount of the engineer and firemen's wages, £3oo, is transferred from the Wages account at the end of the year. The cost of the production of motive power, when added to the Rent and Rates, may be compared with the current prices paid for *room and power,* calculated on the machinery in operation. This comparison will shew whether or not this item of expenditure exceeds the average of other similar concerns *(p). (0)* The stock of material in process of manufacture, and of finished goods, having passed into the transition stage between the raw material purchased and the manufactured goods sold, can be dealt with only as a distinct and special item of the Trading Account. Any difference between the amount of such stock at the commencement and that at the close of a given period must be considered in computing the total consumption or production during that period.

(p) For the information of those who are not acquainted with the manufacturing industries, it may be said that many large mills are occupied by several tenants, the Landlord providing motive power for all and charging rent at so much for each machine.

Rent, Rates, Taxes, Gas and Insurance. Folios 11 and 17, pages 156-7 and 160-1.

Under this head an account is kept for the Mill and another for the Warehouse, which is supposed to be at a distance from the Mill.

In the Trading Account the cost of maintaining the Warehouse is kept distinct from the expenses of manufacture.

Where the premises upon which the business is carried on are owned by the firm a fair rent should be debited to the Trading Account and credited to the Capital Account.

Mill Furnishings *(q)*, Repairs and Renewals Account.

Folio 12, pages 158-9.

The outlay under this head is sub-divided into departments, and the totals of the several columns of the Purchases Day Book are posted to the corresponding columns of this account. The column headed *Store* receives all articles that are not purchased specially for any one department, but which are handed out by the storekeeper as and where required *(e.g.,* Brushes, Strapping, Oilcans, &c.). It is desirable, where convenient, for the purchases of each department to be separately invoiced, in order to avoid the necessity of recording the subsequent distribution.

The stock in each column is supposed to represent only those articles that are already received in the department, but which are not yet handed out for use. The Mill Furnishings in actual use, as well as all other loose utensils, are comprised in the value of the Plant and Machinery in the several departments.

Stables Account. Folio 13, pages 158-9.

All expenditure connected with the stables, including the purchases of *new horses and vehicles,* is charged to this account, and the total of the *carters' and teamers' wages* for the year is transferred from the wages account.

As the values of horses, vehicles, &c., fluctuate very much, and consequently it is not safe to depend upon a fixed rate of depreciation, a new valuation should be made at each stock-taking. The valuation should include horses, vehicles, utensils, provender and all other stable requisites, and the amount of the valuation should be treated as stock on hand. *(q)* The Mill Furnishings, including loose utensils, should be and usually are, kept up to a standard value by replacements, and inasmuch as they do not therefore depreciate in common with the rest of the plant, to be strictly correct, they should be treated as & distinct and separate item. To do this, however, would often involve much complication and difficulty. The ordinary method is to include in one valuation both the Machinery and its necessary complement of Mill Furnishings and Utensils. Depreciation is then caloulated on the whole valuation, and the rate is adjusted so as to allow for that portion wnich is not subject to depreciation. A list of all Mill Furnishings and loose utensils may be kept and compared yearly with the articles actually in use. Any increase or decrease may be then added to, or deducted from, the value of the stock iu store. Bobbins, skeps, *Sec,* should form the subject of a special account in the books of a Spinner (see also *Skep Book).*

The sum transferred to the Trading Account, therefore, represents the total cost of maintaining the stables, which may be compared with the probable cost of hired cartage to perform the same work.

Repairs to Mill Buildings Account. Folio 14, pages 158-9.

The firm, holding the mill under an agreement of tenancy, is responsible for certain repairs, the cost of which is posted to this account.

The cost of new buildings or of improvements to the mill, erected or executed by the tenant and for which the landlord agrees to give compensation at the expiration of the tenancy, should be posted to a distinct account and treated as an asset, subject to depreciation, in the same way as Plant and Machinery. Where the mill is owned by the firm, the cost of new erections or improvements should be posted to the Mill Buildings account, unless it is desired to keep a special account for a particular erection.

Cards Purchases Account. Folio 15, pages 158-9.

Where the carding machinery constitutes a considerable portion of the whole plant, it is essential that the cards should be passed to a separate account, in order that the depreciation may be accurately computed (see *Depreciation).* As a heavy trade discount (often 1o/. or 15) is usually allowed on cards, it should either be deducted from each individual invoice before entering the amount in the Purchases Day Book, or the total discount should be transferred at the end of the year, as in the example.

The balance of this account is transferred to the Private Ledger, where, for the sake of secrecy, the account showing the full valuation of the cards is kept.

Incidental Expenses Account. Folio 16, pages 160-61.

The expenditure under this head at the mill is kept distinct from that at the warehouse by means of two columns. It may be further classified, apart from the books, under several sub-heads, for comparison year by year.

Warehouse and Office Salaries, and Travellers' Salaries and Expenses. Folios 18 and 19, pages 162-3 W

The total payments, only, during each month are entered under these accounts, and the individual salaries and expenses are thus kept secret. The details may be recorded in separate memorandum books.

(r) It is often desirable to compare the results produced by the travellers with their respective salaries and expenses. For this purpose a separate Sales Day book may be kept for each traveller, or additional columns may be provided for classifying the sales. In making comparisons of this character, unless a uniform selling price is strictly adhered to, account should be taken of the profit yielded respectively by the sales of each traveller over and above the cost price of the goods.

Discount on Sales and Discount on Purchases Accounts.

Folios 21 and 22, pages 162—165.

The Discounts on Sales are kept separate from the Discounts on Purchases, for reasons referred to in Chapter VII.

The two items posted to the Cr. side of the Discount on Sales account, and the three items posted to the Dr. side of the Discount on Purchases account, are made up of entries in the Cash Book which are distinguished by the initials S.L. and P.L. against the Ledger folios and which are printed in black type to represent red ink. As to the transfer from the Cards account, see page 214.

Bad Debts Account. Folio 24, pages 164-5.

As already explained on pages 2o5-6, the balance representing the net loss on a bad debt is transferred to this account; also, the whole balance of an insolvent account, the final settlement of which is likely to be prolonged, is transferred, and dividends received in respect thereof are posted to this account.

At the end of the year all debts from which further dividends are expected are valued, and the estimated value is brought down as a balance (see Bentley & Robinson, £59 7s. 7d.) (s).

Plant and Machinery Purchases Account. Folio 25, pages 164-5.

The postings to this account are dissected, and the amount belonging to each department is transferred at the end of the year to the Plant and Machinery account kept in the Private Ledger.

When a deduction is obtained for discount from the price of Plant or Machinery purchased, the amount should be credited to Plant and Machinery account and not to Discount on Purchases account.

We now turn to accounts in the Private Ledger, viz.:—

Plant and Machinery Account, and Cards Account. Folios 1 and 2, pages 182-3.

The purchases both of Machinery and Cards during the year are transferred from the Nominal Ledger, folios 25 and 15. The depreciation in each department is entered in its respective column (a) In order that insolvent accounts may not be overlooked or neglected, when numerous, it is well to post the several items of the Bad Debts account into a small Bad Debts Ledger, kept quite distinct from the ordinary books. Where credit is given to individuals in very large amounts there is often an entire immunity from bad debts for a time, followed by sudden heavy losses. Such losses ought to be provided for in anticipation. A provision fund may be raised by passing yearly to the Cr. of the Bad Debts account a certain percentage (say 10/-per cent.) of the sales. The amount of this percentage is charged to the Dr. of the Trading Account, Section II. All losses are then transferred as they arise to the Bad Debts account, in reduction of the fund. In this way the trading of each year is made to bear an equal burden.

on the Cr. side, and the whole depreciation is charged to the Dr. of the Trading Account, Section II. (page 186). The balances are then brought down, and represent the values in each department at the end of the year.

Income Tax Account. Folio 4, pages 182-3.

This account is re-posted from the Private Ledger account in the Nominal Ledger, folio 31, and the amount is transferred to the Dr. of the Trading Account, Section III.

James Brook, Loan Account. Folio 5, pages 182-3.

This account is re-posted from the Private Ledger account in the Nominal Ledger, folio 31.

The account illustrates the method of recording interest on "Account Current. " The entries of interest, and of the number of days on which it is chargeable, are made in columns alongside the amounts to which they respectively refer, and a balance of interest is struck half-yearly. The half-yearly balances of interest are entered on the Cr. side of the account, and are counterbalanced by entries on the Dr. side of the Interest on Loans and Capital account (f) (see folio 9).

John Blackburn, Loan Account. Folio 6, pages 182-3.

This account is likewise re-posted from the Private Ledger account in the Nominal Ledger.

The account represents *a loan to a relative of one of the partners*. The interest is entered to the Dr. of the account and to the Cr. of the Interest on Lpans and Capital Account (folio 9).

Benjamin Summers and William Blackburn, Capital Accounts. Folios 7 and 8, pages 184-5.

The interest passed to the Cr. of each" of these accounts is carried to the Dr. of Interest on Loans and Capital account.

Interest is often charged upon partners' drawings, but in this case it is assumed that there is an agreement to the contrary, provided they do not exceed a certain sum.

if) If desired, such entries may be made first iu a Journal and then posted therefrom. The Journal entry would be as follows,

Intent on Loans and Capital account, Dr.

To James Brook,

for half-year's interest, as per account current.

However, unless the entries are complicated, the use of the Journal (which has not hitherto been required) is unnecessary and superfluous.

We have now to consider the ARRANGEMENT OF THE TRADING ACCOUNT and the utility of the information to be derived therefrom. The account is divided into three Sections.

Section I. comprises—

On the Cr. side—The Sales, and the Stock at the close of the period.

On the Dr. side—The commencing Stock, the consumption of material and the productive wages.

The items of this section necessarily increase or decrease in proportion to the volume of goods produced.

Section II. comprises—

On the Cr. side—The balance brought down from Section I.

On the Dr. side—The various standing expenses of the business; the manufacturing expenses being kept separate from the non-manufacturing expenses (*i.e.,* the warehouse and office expenses and general charges).

The items of this Section do not necessarily vary, whether the volume of production is more or less.

Section III. shews the manner of distributing the net proceeds of the business.

The items comprised in Section I. can be set out in definite quantities in the calculation of the cost of each individual lot of goods manufactured, while those comprised in Section II. can only be stated in the form of a general average based on the whole production (see Cost books) («).

The balance of Section I. represents the surplus realised from goods sold, over and above the cost of material and wages employed in their manufacture. If the cost prices, rates of wages and sale prices are relatively the same, this balance should year by year represent a similar percentage of the Sales, whether they be more or less. (In the example the percentage is 27). Therefore, any change in this percentage indicates an increase or decrease in the rate of profit obtained on the goods sold, *as a result of altered prices.*

Any variation in the Standing Expenditure under Section 11., unless accounted for by a large increase or decrease of production, or other exceptional cause, indicates economy or extravagance in the working expenses.

(«) The correspondence between the aggregates of the Trading Account and the individual cost calculations is more clearly shewn in the Departmental accounts hereafter described.

It is obvious that a certain amount of trade must be done before working expenses are earned. After that minimum is passed, any reasonable addition to the sales, at the same prices, will increase the surplus of Section I. without appreciably adding to the expenses under Section II.

The Trading Account arranged in this form, therefore, not only shews the details and the result of past trading, but may be utilised in prospecting the effect upon future profits of any of the following modifications in the business arrangements, viz:— (i.) An increase or decrease of the turnover; affecting chiefly Section I.
(ii.) An increase or decrease of the sale prices; affecting Section I. (iii.) An extension or curtailment of the means of selling goods; affecting both Sections I. and II.

The expense, or the saving, of a traveller's or agent's salary, commission, &c., is set off against the gain or loss resulting from the alteration in the turnover.
(iv.) An extension or curtailment of the means of producing goods, or of the branches or articles of manufacture.

Section I. would be affected by the altered turnover.

Section II. would be affected by any alteration in the means of selling, consequent upon the altered turnover, also by alterations in supervision, as well as in maintaining and turning machinery, &c.

The following items of the Trading Account require separate consideration, viz.:— DISCOUNT ON SALES.—This item is stated under the head of General Charges. It varies according to the volume of trade, but it is not included under Section I. because it is largely affected by the terms of credit granted to customers and their mode of payment. In computing the sale price of goods the full discount (usually 7. per cent.) should be allowed for as a distinct deduction.

DISCOUNT on PURCHASES.—This item also varies according to the volume of trade, but is largely affected by the financial resources of the firm. In calculating the cost of goods manufactured it is usual to charge the full invoice price of material, plus the expenses of transit, brokerage, &c., without regard to discount which may or may not be obtained. This method is fully justified by the fact that the material is often bought and paid for many months before the goods manufactured from it are delivered. BANK CHARGES are affected by many of the same considerations as Discounts, and are likewise stated under the head of General Charges. Both Discounts and Bank Charges receive further attention subsequently (see *Finance).* BAD DEBTS.—This item of course fluctuates, except where a Provision Fund is created, as referred to on page 215, note (s). DEPARTMENTAL ACCOUNTS.

The treatment of this important subject falls naturally into two division:— (i.) Selling Departments.
(ii.) Manufacturing Departments.

Selling Departments.

On pages 192-3 is given a specimen Departmental Trading Account (note *v,* page 222), where the firm is supposed to manufacture and sell both yarn and cloth. The three columns respectively show the details and the result of the trading—(i.) of the Yarn Department, (ii.) of the Cloth Department, (iii.) of the whole concern.

To compile this account it is obvious that the various items of income and expenditure, as well as the Stock in each department, must be kept distinct and separate. To do this it is often desirable in large concerns, to keep entirely distinct sets of books, but all that is actually necessary is to separate the details from which the nominal accounts are made up. For instance, each department should have its own Day Books for Purchases, Sales, and Returns, or at any rate these books must be provided with distinct columns for each department. If only one Cash Book is employed, the discounts must be analysed so that the proper amount may be charged to each department, and the Cash Book may be provided with extra columns for this purpose. The discounts may, however, often be divided with sufficient accuracy by charging each department with the ordinary rates allowed on its total purchases and sales. A record must be kept of all goods supplied by one selling department to another, and the Trading Account of each must be charged with the amount, whether for or against. Thus, in the example, the Yarn Department is credited with the amount of yarn supplied to the Cloth Department, viz., "15,116 17s. iod., and the Cloth Department is debited with the like amount.

Manufacturing Departments.

Before describing the preparation of accounts disclosing the profit or loss on the different processes of manufacture, it may be well to clear the way by pointing out certain unfeasible ideas that occur to many book-keepers whose experience is only theoretic, and which usually end in the abandonment of their whole project as hopelessly complicated.

In the first place, accounts of Manufacturing Departments should be entirely *supplemental* to the Trading Account, and they should neither interfere with, nor form part of the ordinary book-keeping. Much unnecessary complication is introduced into a comparatively simple operation when the details of the Departmental Accounts are mixed up with the books of the counting-house. The intention of including everything in one comprehensive system of double-entry is perfectly right, but the method is altogether injudicious.

Secondly, it is impracticable, as well as useless, to charge each successive department with the value of the goods supplied to it from other departments.

The only plan which is thoroughly workable and satisfactory is briefly as follows:—

The foreman of each department keeps a record of work done in the processes under his supervision, and the profit or loss is ascertained by comparing in each case the value of such *work* done, when calculated at trade prices (note *w,* page 222), with the proportion of wages and expenses chargeable against the respective department.

Therefore, in addition to the Trading Account, Sections I. and II. (see pages 186-7), all that is required in order to ascertain the profit or loss of the Manufacturing Departments is:— (i.) A record of work done in each department.
(ii.) A departmental analysis of the expenditure comprised in Sections I. and II. of the Trading Account.
The method of ascertaining the amount of work done in each department is described on pages 256-7.

The analysis of expenditure is very easily obtained and on page 196 a specimen Summary of the analysis is given. The headings of the several columns of the Summary indicate the divisions under which the whole expenditure of the concern is to be apportioned.

The column headed GOODS receives the value of the Stock of Goods finished and in process of manufacture at the commencement of the year, also the cost of Raw Material consumed, the cost of Outwork (note *x* page 222), Packing Materials and Carriage (note *y,* page 222); in other words, the commencing Stock and the total cost of Material consumed in producing the manufactured article.

The five succeeding columns receive their respective apportionments of expenditure chargeable against the several processes of manufacture carried on in the mill (note *z,* page 222).

The column headed PATTERN MAKING provides for a distinct and special item of expenditure which, in certain branches of trade, such as high-class worsted manufacturing, is often very large (note *a,* page 223).

The standing expenses of the warehouse and office and the general charges are not connected with the departments of manufacture, and it is unnecessary therefore to analyse them.

Having before us (i.) the Trading Account, Sections I. and II., (ii.) the value of Work Done in the several departments, (iii.) the Departmental Analysis of the expenditure, we can prepare therefrom, without reference to any other accounts whatever, the Manufacturing Account, Sections I. and II. (see pages 194-5).

The Manufacturing Account, Section I., shews—

On the Cr. side—The year's Sales, and the remaining Stock.

On the Dr. side—(i.) The commencing Stock, and the total cost of Material consumed during the year, obtained from column 2 of the analysis, page 196.
(ii.) The expenses of Pattern Making, obtained from column 8 of the analysis, page 196. (iii.) The charge for Processes of Manufacture at trade prices, obtained from the record of work done.

The difference between the Dr. and Cr. sides is transferred to the Cr. of Section II., as the *gross selling profit,* and corresponds in the aggregate with the margin allowed in calculating the prices of goods, between the *cost of production* and the *sale price.* The method of calculating piece goods is explained on page 254 (see *Piece Cost Book).*

The Manufacturing Account, Section I., which is in effect an aggregation of the individual cost calculations, proves conclusively whether those calculations, as a whole, have been realised (note *b,* page 223).

Any insufficiency in the *margin* or balance of this account, if not the result of incorrect calculations, can only arise from one of two causes, either that the manufactured goods have been sold *too cheaply,* or that the raw material from which they have been made has been purchased *too dearly* (note *c,* page 223). The insufficiency should, therefore, have been anticipated while making the individual calculations.

It should be clearly understood that this insufficiency cannot be attributed to unprofitable working of the processes of manufacture, as each process is charged at the standard trade price and not at its actual cost.

The Manufacturing Account, Section II., shews—

On the Cr. side—(i.) The gross *selling profit,* transferred from Section I.
(ii.) The profit on the several processes or departments of manufacture *(i.e.,* the Manufacturing or Machinery profit).
(iii.) The Discount on Purchases, which is so much earned by the counting-house through its financial arrangements.

On the Dr. side—The Warehouse and Office standing expenses, and the General Charges.

The difference between the Dr. and Cr. sides represents the net earnings of the entire concern, and corresponds with the balance of Section II. of the Trading Account, pages 186-7.

The profit on the Processes of Manufacture is ascertained as follows:—The value of Work done under each process, which has been charged to the Dr. of Section I., is entered in the Cr. column. The amount of the Wages and Expenses of each process, obtained from the Analysis, page 196, is entered in the Dr. column. The difference in each department represents the profit. Inasmuch as in this account each department receives credit for its work at the standard prices accepted by those who carry on its special process as a distinct trade, it should, other things being equal, gain the usual rate of profit. It sometimes happens, however, that a department is not fully employed, or is worked under other disadvantages, and any such special reason for non-success must be taken into consideration.

NOTES REFERRED TO ON PAGES 219-221. (v) The specimen Trading Account is based on the figures of that on pages 186-7, but the relative capacities of the various manufacturing departments would, of course, be altogether different. (vo) There is a well-known trade price for almost every process of manufacture (i.e. a price at which the goods can be put out to work) In Yorkshire the term *country work* prices will be understood. (x) Outwork includes all processes put out to work, whether by reason of pressure of trade, or because the special process is not carried on in the mill, and the amount is treated as extra cost of material.

Where the articles manufactured by the firm are all of one class, passing through exactly the same processes, the cost of Outwork may be sub-divided and added to the work of the same character done in the several departments. The total cost of each process whether done in the mill or outside, may thus be compared with the whole production year by year.

Where, however, the goods manufactured are of many different kinds, this comparison, other than in detail, will be valueless, as the cost of the respective processes will vary with the nature of the goods. For instance a manufacturer, of plain black cloth might compare the total cost of dyeing with the total goods produced, but such a comparison would be useless to a manufacturer of fancy goods, as the prices for dyeing vary largely according to colours.

(y) Packing Material is usually invoiced with the goods and afterwards returned and allowed for. It may, in some instances, more conveniently appear in Section II. as a warehouse expense. Carriage may, or may not, be paid on goods purchased, and likewise ou goods sold. That paid on goods purchased properly belongs to Section I., and that on goods sold may be treated as a warehouse expense under Section II. The arrangement of these items is determined by the custom of the particular business, but should be made to correspond with the cost calculations. (;) The headings of departments in the illustration are simply typical, and the extent and nature of the sub-division must depend entirely upon the class of business, and its own peculiarities. It is sufficient that the principle is essentially the same in all cases.

Many of the items of the Trading Account can be apportioned to the several processes without sub-division in detail, others are already dissected in the Purchases Day Book and Nominal Ledger.

The storekeeper who has charge of the materials and stores, such as CHEMICALS, SOAP, OIL, 4c, which are often purchased in bulk for use in more than one department, must make periodical returns to the counting-house of the quantities supplied by him to each. Instead of the heading Chemicals, Soap, Oil, c, it is often, but not always, convenient to adopt the following heads, viz. :—(i) Scouring or Milling Requisites, (ii.) Finishing Requisites, (iii.) Size, which is chargeable to the Weaving Department, (iv.) Manufacturing Oil. The latter is used for mixing with the material, and may be extended into the Goods column of the Analysis, page 196. These headings, when adopted, shew the amount chargeable to each department without further analysis.

For the sub-division of WAGES (see *Wages*, pages 241-6).

Time sheets may be kept by the MECHANICS, JOINERS, AND PLUMBERS, and their wages may be apportioned according to the time occupied.

The cost of MOTIVE POWER may be charged according to the machinery turned in each department, or, if preferred, the Bent, Bates, and Taxes and the cost of Motive Power may be combined, and the whole sum apportioned according to the Boom and Power occupied. There is a well-known standard price for Boom and Power in manufacturing districts, reckoned at so much per machine. A separate account is sometimes kept to shew the profit or loss resulting to the firm as owners of the mill and providers of Boom and Power.

The floor area of the mill may be subdivided to form the basis for apportioning the BENT, BATES, AND TAXES when treated separately. The number of GAS lights in each department may be counted, or, better still, separate meters may be used.

The FIRE INSUBANCE is usually apportioned in the Policy.

MILL FUBNISHINGS And BEPAIRS And EENEWALS To MACHINERY are dissected in the Purchases Day Book and Nominal Ledger (see pages 82—93 and 168-9), except those articles which are purchased in bulk for use in several departments, and which are extended into the column headed *Store*.

In small concerns the whole sum of the items in the *Store* column may be apportioned by estimate, but, where convenient, the storekeeper should record the quantities issued by him to each department *(tee Mill Furnishings, ,1V., Stock Hook)*. MILL BUILDING REPAIBS may usually be apportioned from the accounts rendered by those who do the work.

The DEPBECIATION in departments has been already referred to on page 216.

Where it is desired to institute a system of Departmental Accounts, it will be found convenient for many things previously purchased and invoiced in bulk to be separately invoiced, and little difficulty will be experienced in getting this done if proper directions are given to the vendors when the orders are placed.

Although estimates should be avoided where possible, it must be borne in mind that, while substantial accuracy is neccessary, account keeping of this character should never require the employment of superfluous clerical labour in recording minute details that do not materially affect the result. The ordinary staff of a well-organised mill, if properly directed, can do all that is essential for the preparation of Departmental Accounts on the principle here described.

(a) It will be observed that only the wages and expenses of Pattern Making are set out in this column, no separate account being taken of the yarn consumed.

To ascertain the total outlay, a record must be kept of the yarn used and the cost thereof added to the wages and expenses. From such total outlay the amount realised from patterns sold, as shewn in the Pattern Day Book, must be deducted—tluis £ s. d.

Wages and expenses, us per analysis, page 196 1337 3 4

Cost of yarn (say) 700 0 0 2037 3 4

Less Patterns sold as per Pattern Day Book—

March 310 0 i

September.. 342 4 7

Net cost £1384 18 3

Where it is not convenient to record the exact quantities of yarn handed over to the Pattern Department, the cost may be roughly computed by weighing the patterns made and charging the yarn at so much per lb.

(6) In comparing the margin of profit shown by the manufacturing account with the average margin shown by the individual calculations, the loss on goods sold at job prices, or at prices under those fixed, must be taken into account. It is well to keep a record of the loss so arising. (c) An undue proportion of waste of material in the process of manufacture would, of course, diminish the margin of profit, but, except in cases of gross negligence, the excess of waste would not materially affect the result. A rigid check should, however, alwayfa be imposed upon the relative yield of material from the different workpeople.

RECAPITULATION.

It may be well here to recapitulate the uses and advantages of the information obtained from both the Trading Account and the Departmental Accounts.

(i.) Section I. of the Trading Account, pages 186-7, shews the surplus earned from goods sold, over and above the cost of raw material and productive wages. This surplus, when compared as a *percentage of the sales* with accounts of previous periods, indicates any change in the rate of profit upon goods sold, and is particularly useful when departmental accounts are not kept. (ii.) Section Il. of the Trading Account shews the standing expenses of the business classified under the most important heads, so that any increase or decrease may be detected by comparing the expenditure of each class with that of previous periods. (iii.) From the information given in both Sections I. and II. of the Trading Account may be calculated the probable advantages that will accrue from any possible increase of the sales. The surplus of Section l. will increase or decrease in proportion with the sales, while the standing expenditure of Section II. may or may not vary, according to the circumstances of the case. (iv.) The Manufacturing Account, Section I., pages 194-5, shews the gross selling profit, or, in other words, the aggregate margin of profit obtained after deducting the *cost of manufacture (d)* from the *sale* price. (v.) The Manufacturing Account, Section II., shews whether the individual processes or departments of manufacture are being carried on economically, in other words, shews the *Machinery* profit or loss.

These accounts also furnish full information as to the cost of *Warehousing, Distribution, and Finance.*

The experience of an Accountant, who has extensive practice amongst manufacturers, enables him to determine the precise rates of percentage and margins of profit, in respect of the foregoing accounts, that prevail in the various classes of trade for the time being.

When it is remembered that a very small miscalculation or omission in fixing prices, or careless and incompetent supervision in one or more departments, will often change a handsome profit into a serious loss, the importance of the information which may be derived from *skilled* manipulation of these accounts is obvious. In disclosing with certainty the *exact cause of every fluctuation of profit or loss,* they may be said to answer every object for which account keeping of this character is designed.

(d) The calculation of the coBt of making the goods being based on what other concerns of a like nature are charging for the processes, all doubt is removed as to the sufficiency of the sale prices. The actual cost of manufacture may, and often does, exceed the standard charges, but such increased cost will appear as a loss in the departments; it does not add to the selling value of the goods. In cases where a business has paid well in the past, but the profits of which have declined for causes not entirely perceptible, the application of these accounts has often rendered great assistance in diagnosing the ailments of the concern. The secret of declining profits has been revealed and in several instances this discovery has had the effect of restoring prosperity to a failing business. It is, however, essential that the person who is called upon for advice of this character should thoroughly understand the organisation and working of the business, practically as well as financially. Others will stumble at almost every step over obstacles which are easily surmounted by those who know the nature of the ground that they have to traverse.

In leaving this subject it may be stated that the plan above described, modified to suit particular requirements, has for many years been in successful operation in almost every class of Textile Manufacturing, and that it is carried out with perfect ease, even in concerns of the most intricate character. Therefore, if the general outline of the plan be properly understood, it may be taken for granted there will be no insuperable difficulty in the details of its application.

Before closing this chapter it may be well to offer a few remarks as to VOLUME AND VALUE OF PRODUCTION,

AND DECIMAL CALCULATIONS.

In nearly all manufacturing concerns it is desirable to take account of the *volume,* as well as of the value of the goods produced, and to compare the one with the other. Prices often fluctuate considerably, and more expensive goods may be manufactured in one period than in another. Therefore, if values alone are regarded, misleading conclusions may be arrived at.

It is generally inexpedient to introduce quantities into the financial books, although it may be done with advantage in simple cases. Perhaps the simplest manufacturing accounts are those of a Cotton Spinner who produces one class of yarn, and there is no objection to placing the weights of raw cotton bought in the Purchases Day Book and carrying forward the total weights into the Cotton Purchases Account in the Nominal Ledger. The weights sold may also be cast up in the Sales Day Book and entered in the Sales Account. By adjusting the weights in stock at the commencement and at the end of the given period, the total consumption of raw material, and the total production of yarn may thus be shewn both in volume and value.

Where varieties of yarn are produced it is necessary to classify the quantities of each, and this cannot be conveniently done in the financial books.

The cost of the various items of expenditure, per piece or per lb. of the production, is much more readily compared with the corresponding figures of other periods when reduced to decimals.

Thus, the weight of yarn produced may be (say) 1,oo1,272 lbs., value "36,5o4 14s. 2d., or 8"75od. per lb.; the cost of raw material "21,381 6s. 7d., or 5"i25d. per lb. of yarn produced; the cost of wages "6779 8s. nd., or t-625d. per lb. of yarn produced; and so on with the other expenditure.

These decimal figures may be placed alongside of the several items of the Trading Account, either of the whole concern or of its several departments. Where the expenses cannot be calculated on the basis of the *quantity* they may be reckoned as percentages of the *value* of goods produced.

It must be remembered that the comparison of expenditure with either the volume or value of the production *as a whole* is more or less unreliable, according to the variety of the production. This applies equally to the Spinner and the Manufacturer. If more than one department is carried on the expenses of each should be considered separately, as the work of the given period may require more expense in one and less in another, although the quantity or value of the whole production may remain about the same.

It may here be repeated that the only method of testing the economy of manufacturing departments that the author has found to be altogether satisfactory and reliable is that already described; viz., Credit each department with standard prices for its work done, and Debit it with its proportion of the expenditure.

CHAPTER V.

Special And Auxiliary Books.

Subject to minor modifications, the general system of book-keeping explained in the preceding pages is suitable for all departments of manufacture, whether carried on collectively or individually. According to requirements, however, the headings of the classification columns of the Purchases Day Book, the titles of the Nominal Accounts, and the ruling of the Sales Day Book, must be varied, while certain transactions peculiar to departments require special and auxiliary books.

Commission Workers, *i.e.,* Dyers, Extractors, Combers, Scribblers, Spinners, Weavers, Finishers and others who receive goods to be worked by them on commission, require special books for recording *Goods Received* and *Goods Delivered,* although the Day Book often supplies the place of the latter.

These books should be ruled *(e)* so as to set out the following particulars, viz:—

Goods Received Book.—Date received—name and description— quantity of material or distinctive number of piece—work to be done —folio of Goods Delivered Book where the delivery is entered.

Goods Delivered Book.—Date delivered—name and description —quantity or piece No.—Folio of Goods Received Book.

A Dyer, Finisher, or other worker of piece goods should give his own number to each piece received. Such numbers should follow in consecutive order in the Goods Received Book, and should be recorded, together with the customer's number, throughout the bookkeeping where necessary for identification.

A Delivery Note Book may often be utilised in place of the Goods Delivered Book.

The delivery notes should be numbered consecutively, and perforated so that they may be easily torn out. Duplicate leaves, also numbered, but not perforated, should alternate with the perforated leaves to receive impressions from carbon paper. The duplicates remaining in the covers form a permanent record of all deliveries, and from them the invoices or accounts may be written up periodically in the Day Book.

(e) It is impracticable here to give specimens of the many varieties of rulings required for different branches of manufacture. So long as the above-mentioned essential particulars are provided for, any further columns may be added according to requirement.

It is often necessary to classify the deliveries of goods before they are entered in the Day Book, especially in the following circumstances, viz:— (i.) Where the items are very numerous, as in the case of a Piece Dyer or Finisher. (ii.) Where the charge for work done cannot be computed until all the deliveries of one description are complete. (iii.) Where the *net* weight cannot be ascertained until the *tare* has been returned *(e.g.,* Spinners' skeps and bobbins).

In circumstances such as above indicated, it is usual to forward a delivery note with each delivery, and to furnish a monthly or quarterly account in lieu of invoices.

The classification of deliveries, whether of work done or of goods supplied, is conveniently effected by means of a

Detail Ledger (/), which is ruled in precisely the same form as the Day Book. As in the case of an ordinary Ledger, a number of pages are appropriated to each customer, and the particulars of all deliveries are regularly posted thereto from the Delivery Book or from the counterfoils of the Delivery Notes.

When the monthly or quarterly accounts are required to be furnished, the deliveries are priced out and cast up in the Detail Ledger. The account furnished to the customer, which is made up from the Detail Ledger, may, if desired, be press-copied, and the total only need be entered in the Day Book, reference being made for particulars either to the page of the press-copy book or of the Detail Ledger, or of both.

Great care should be exercised to ensure that no deliveries are overlooked, and that the postings and calculations in the Detail Ledger are properly verified. It must be remembered that both the Delivery Books and the Detail Ledger are merely auxiliaries to the Day Book, and the balancing of the ordinary books imposes no check upon them.

Tare Records.—In several departments of manufacture it is essential to keep records of the delivery and return of Tares *g)*, and this is of the utmost importance to a Spinner who delivers yarn on spools or bobbins. A special book is sometimes employed, but where convenient both the goods and the tares should be combined in one entry. The Detail Ledger is a very convenient medium for this purpose, and the following form with slight modifications is used by several large Spinners:— (/) The Detail Ledger is very suitable for Engineers and Machinists, whose work consists largely of repairs.

(;/) The word tare signifies the *deduction* from the gross weight, but the plural form is employed here in the sense in which it is commonly used, and denotes *the articles* iu respect of which the deduction is made.

Form of DETAIL LEDGER for SPINNERS who deliver yarn on spools or bobbins.

The Spinner usually forwards a delivery note with each delivery, and furnishes an account to his customer at the end of the month. The particulars of each delivery are posted from the duplicate delivery note to the Detail Ledger. A *credit note,* or acknowledgment, is given to the customer for every return of tares. The credit notes are in duplicate, like the delivery notes, and from the duplicates the particulars of the returns are posted alongside the deliveries to which they respectively relate. When the skeps, spools, or bobbins are not returned before the invoice or monthly account is made out, the tare is usually estimated and entered in red ink. The items of the account are then calculated and extended into the money columns. When the actual tare is eventually ascertained, any difference between the estimated and the actual weight is extended into the *Debit or Credit Tare* column, as the case may be, and is added to or deducted from a subsequent account. This method is very simple and concise; it is perfectly safe, and it avoids many complications in the ordinary Ledger.

SALES LEDGER for dividing SEASONS' GOODS.

The Woollen and Worsted and other cloth trades have two seasons— Spring and Winter—and much difficulty in ruling off the Ledger accounts is caused by the peculiar terms of payment. In order to enable each settlement to be clearly defined, several large firms have adopted a Ledger specially ruled to divide the seasons' goods. The form is as follows:—

Form of SALES LEDGER for dividing SEASONS' GOODS. *Dr. Cr.*

As each settlement is made the items are cast up, whether in the Spring or the Winter column, and the amount is extended into the total column and ruled off. Intermediate or current goods are posted in either the Spring or the Winter column, whichever may for the time being be vacant. As to Seasons' Patterns, see page 2oo.

Another form of CASH BOOK.

The form of Cash book given on the following page is better suited to the requirements of some concerns than that given in the example pages 1o6—127, although it involves a little more work.

All moneys received, whether retained in hand or deposited in the bank, are entered on the left-hand side in the *Cash* column, and the total amount of each deposit into the bank is entered in the *Bank* column. All moneys paid, whether out of cash in hand or out of the bank, by cheque or otherwise, are entered on the right-hand side in the *Cash* column, and if paid out of the bank the amount is also entered in the *Bank* column.

In order to balance the cash, the right-hand Bank column is cast up, and the amount.(4o16 4s. 9d.) is entered in the left-hand Cash column as so much *received from the bank,* and the left-hand Bank column is cast up and the amount (8135 14s. od.) is entered in the right-hand Cash column, as so much *paid into the bank.* The difference between the left-hand and right-hand Cash columns then shews the amount of cash in hand. The transverse entries of the totals of the Bank columns are posted to the Bank Account in the Nominal Ledger, from which the balance at the bank is ascertained when required. If preferred, however, the commencing Bank balance may be entered in the Bank column of the Cash Book, so that the state of the Bank Account may be ascertained without reference to the Ledger. When this is done the commencing balance must not be included in the total entered in the opposite Cash column.

The transactions recorded in this form are identical with those on pages 1o6-7 so far as January 13th. The two methods may therefore be compared, and the cash balance struck on that date will be found to be the same in both forms.

The extra columns for *Totals Posted* may be added where required.

CHAPTER VI.

Depreciation *(h).* It is intended to deal with this subject only so far as it relates to those classes of property usually connected with manufacturing concerns *(e. g.,* Mills, Warehouses, Leases, Plant, Machinery, Utensils, Furniture and Fixtures).

It may be regarded as a broad principle that *existing Works, Plant, Machinery, &c, should be efficiently maintained by all necessary repairs and renewals, out of revenue, and, in addition, the Trading Account should bear an adequate charge for* depreciation.

Amongst the causes of depreciation may be mentioned the following, viz:—
(i.) Supersession by improvements.
(ii.) Reduction in cost of labour and material,
(iii.) Decline in profits,
(iv.) Wear and tear.

The effect of causes i., ii. and iii. cannot be estimated in anticipation, and the measure of provision in respect thereof must be wholly determined by prudential considerations.

The effect of *Wear and Tear,* although subject to no precise rules, can be fairly approximated.

The assessment of the charge for depreciation differs according to the nature of the property. The following observations point out the peculiarities of each class.

Buildings.—The quality and durability of the structure of Buildings of all kinds must be considered. Local fluctuations in value of property may cause either appreciation or depreciation. It is recommended that changes in value from this cause should be adjusted by actual valuation. An *unearned increment* arising therefrom is a suitable element for a reserve fund; on the other hand, it is usually advisable to write off a decrease of value, either straightway or by instalments over a number of years.

MILL BUILDINGS cannot well be dissevered from their fixed motive powers, fixed power machinery (I), and steam, gas, and water pipes, inasmuch as without these the building itself is incomplete, and cannot properly be designated a Mill. Moreover, both the building and motive plant are affected for the most part by like causes of depreciation. It is true engines and boilers may be replaced while the building remains, but owing to the radical alterations in structure, necessitated by improvements in machinery, the design of the building (A) It is entirely beyond the scope of this treatise to discuss the many polemical issues of the subject of depreciation. The present intention is simply to afford information of a strictly practical character, and to point out methods, admittedly empirical rather than scientific, which experience has shown to be reliable. (t) The Bills of Sale Act, 1878, furnishes the following definitions:—Fixed motive powers comprise water wheels, steam engines, steam boilers and donkey engines. Fixed power machinery comprises shafts, wheels, drums, and their fixed appurtenances which transmit the action of the motive powers to the other machinery. is often obsolete as soon as the motive plant is worn out. If preferred, however, the depreciation of the building may be treated separately from that of the motive plant. When a new engine or boiler is laid down, the cost thereof, less the value (realised by sale) of that which it replaces, should be added to the *Capital* value, but all repairs should be charged against *Revenue*.

Leases.—The depreciation in value of a lessee's interest in property held for a term of years may be calculated:— (i.) By dividing the purchase money, or original value, by the number of years of the term; the product representing one year's depreciation. By this method the earlier years bear the heavier burden, inasmuch as the interest on the capital invested in the lease is not taken into account, and such interest decreases year by year as the value of the lease diminishes. (ii.) By finding the amount which, if charged annually, will exhaust the value at the expiration of the lease, after taking credit for interest on the annual balances at a fixed rate *(J)*.

This method is more exact than the preceding one, as the charge for depreciation is equally divided over the whole term, and the amount taken to credit for interest on the capital invested in the lease is diminished year by year as the value of the lease decreases.

Although it is often perfectly justifiable to take credit for interest, the former method is recommended in ordinary cases, on the ground that it is always wise to be on the safe side and to charge the revenue with a little extra in the present in order to provide for a lighter burden in the future. Moreover, by way of compensation, repairs are often heavier at the end than at the commencement of the term. Special provision should be made when the lease contains a dilapidation clause.

(j) From Inwood's Tables, or other similar work, select the table shewing the *value in years' purchase* of an annuity (or lease) at the required rate of interest. Divide the value of the lease by the years' purchase shown by the table, and the product represents the amount to be written off annually as depreciation, Interest on the annual balances will, of course, be passed to the Dr. of the Lease Account and the Cr. of the Interest on Capital Account.

Thus:—The value at 6% interest of a lease (or annuity) of £1 for three years is '2·723 (years' purchase). Assume the present value of the lease at £1000—1000 ·2·723 = 367 21 = £367 4s. 2d.

The Ledger Account of the Lease would be as follows:—

Plant and Machinery.—The depreciation of Plant and Machinery may be assessed by any of the following methods, viz:— (i.) Re-valuation; the amount of depreciation being the difference between the old and new valuations, after allowing for additions meanwhile.

(ii.) The deduction of a fixed amount yearly from the cost of each individual machine; the aggregate deduction being written off from the value of the plant as a whole.

This method involves much labour, but it is often carried out in order to know the exact value of the machinery in each room in case of partial destruction by fire. The account may be kept in the following form, of course apart from the ordinary book-keeping

The book may be ruled with as many columns as may be desired.

Fractions of a pound should either be omitted altogether or stated in decimals.

For the purpose of identification, the machines should be labelled with a number corresponding with the number in the account.

Any number of machines of exactly the same type and age may be calculated in the aggregate.

(iii.) Having ascertained the probable working life of the machinery as a whole (or in each department) and the residual value at the expiration of the life, deduct the residual value from the first cost and divide by the number of years of the expected life; the product may be written off annually as depreciation until the residual value is reached.

By this method all additional machinery must be depreciated separately, as the value thereof will be exhausted at different dates.

(iv.) Having ascertained the probable working life of the machinery and the value, if any, when it is worn out, charge a percentage upon the diminishing value sufficient to reduce the first cost to the residual value by the time when the working life expires.

The last method (iv.) is the simplest, and the percentages may be adjusted with sufficient accuracy (see Table, page 236).

The following Table is compiled from the author's experience of a large number of cases:—

In fixing the above rates of depreciation, it is assumed that the machinery will be kept running during the hours prescribed by the Factory Acts: overtime or short time must be allowed for. It is also assumed that the machinery will be kept in efficient repair. An independent valuation every five years may be made, where convenient, as a check upon the system of depreciation.

Cards (k)—Where the Carding machinery constitutes a considerable portion of the whole plant it is very desirable that a distinct account should be kept of the Cards. The average working life of Cards is from five to seven years, according to their quality and the character of work on which they are employed. The simplest and most effective method of keeping the account is to add all expenditure to the capital value, and to write off annually from one-fifth to oneseventh of the cost of clothing completely all the machines in operation. The Cards covering certain parts of the machines wear out much more rapidly than others, and if desired the account may be so ruled as to divide the outlay under several heads *(e.g.,* Swifts, Doffers, Strippers, Angles, Workers, and Fancies). Varying rates of depreciation may then be written off, according to the average length of life of each class. Elaborate details of this character are, however, more conveniently dealt with outside the financial books.

(k) Woollen Cards are especially referred to here, but Worsted and Cotton Cards may be treated in like manner. SO

CHAPTER VII.

Finance And Duties Of The Cashier.

The management of the finances of a manufacturing business requires much skill and forethought.

Considerable sacrifices are often made by small capitalists in raising funds to meet engagements which ought never to be contracted, or which, with proper management, might be provided for without loss. Others with ample resources are careless as to the manipulation of the funds at their command, and consequently neglect a very fruitful source of income.

In order to finance to the best advantage it is necessary to know in advance what funds will be available in the immediate future. For this purpose the cashier should compile a table shewing in monthly totals what accounts are expected to be received and what are contracted to be paid.

A small increase of Capital or overdraft at the bank will sometimes enable a firm to take discounts, by prompt payment, which they would otherwise loose. Where the terms of payment, as in the Woollen trade, allow the option, after a clear month's credit, of a four month's bill, or prompt cash less 2I per cent., such an increase of available money will produce 7 per cent, per annum.

The terms of a banking account are entirely subject to arrangement, and vary very much according to locality, the nature and comparative safety of the account, and other circumstances. A Yorkshire banker may, and usually does, offer the following terms to a manufacturer, viz:—To charge interest at the rate of 5 per cent, upon an overdraft, and to allow interest at the rate of ito 2J per cent, (according to the value of money) upon a credit balance; bills (if first class) to be discounted at the Bank rate for the time being for accounts having a credit balance, and at a half per cent, above the Bank rate for accounts having an overdraft. A commission to be charged upon the *turnover* of one-quarter per cent, while the account is overdrawn, and one-eighth per cent, while there is a credit balance.

The financial manager of the firm should constantly watch and anticipate the state of the Bank account, striving where possible to keep a balance to credit, and thus avoid the double charges of an overdraft. He will often have to make very careful calculations in order to decide whether a greater advantage, present or future, will be gained by giving an acceptance or by paying prompt cash.

Where an acceptance is given the customary 7. per cent, discount is sometimes allowed, less the Bank rate for discounting the bill. Inasmuch as the Bank rate averages only 2 to 3 per cent, this method of payment is obviously a decided advantage to the payer, although it may properly be refused by the payee on the ground that he has to run the risk of four month's longer credit without compensation. Where, however, the status of the payer is beyond doubt, the payee receives exactly the same as though he were paid prompt cash less 2 per cent., and has consequently no cause for complaint (/).

Bills received from customers may be kept in hand until they mature, or may be discounted at any time prior to maturity. The expediency of either holding or discounting depends upon the funds available, the rate of discount, and the state of the firm's Bank account for the time being. Inasmuch as the discount rate only averages from 2 to 3 per cent., it is clearly more profitable to discount all bills received, than, by keeping them in hand, to necessitate a permanent increase of Capital or bank overdraft.

Bills are frequently discounted with bill brokers and other discount houses in order to obtain a lower rate, but the extra trouble involved in this course is seldom compensated by the benefit derived therefrom. The Banker should first be approached for better terms.

As to dealing with Foreign Bills, see *Bills of Exchange,* in the Appendix. It is a safe and desirable practice to pass all money (excepting small sums), both received and paid, through the bank. The paying away of customers' cheques in discharge of debts owing by the firm in order to save bank commission, generally speaking, is false economy and is open to many objections. Whilst a cheque is in circulation interest on the amount is lost, the drawer may fail, and opportunities for fraud are multiplied. On the other hand, payment by the firm's own cheque or by banker's draft decreases the chances of embezzlement, furnishes undeniable evidence of the amount paid, and facilitates the book-keeping. Payment by banker's draft at 14 or 21 days is often accepted instead of cash, and the bank commission is thus saved. Where banker's drafts for large sums are received by the firm, they may sometimes with advantage be paid away before they become due. The draft should be endorsed to the order of the party to whom it is paid.

The prompt collection of outstanding debts is a matter of much importance. The cashier should call attention to all overdue accounts (() The following instance will suffice to illustrate the important advantages to be gained by this mode of payment:—A firm purchasing material amounting annually to about £90,000 was in the habit of paying prompt cash, less 2J per cent, discount. The firm borrowed £60,000 at 6 per cent, interest as loan capital, a portion of which was suddenly recalled at the death of one of the parties. In order to provide funds to meet this demand payment by bills on the above principle was resorted to, and was eventually accepted by all houses from whom goods were purchased. The result of this change in the mode of payment was as follows, viz:—The £90,000 per annum was paid by acceptances at four months instead of prompt cash, consequently £30,000 in bills was continually outstanding, and of course the same amount of Capital was released to pay off the loan. The customary 2J per cent, discount was obtained as before, less the Bank rate for discounting the bills which averaged 2§ per cent, per annum. The difference, therefore, between the 6 per cent, interest previously paid on the loan capital and the 2f per cent, allowed for discounting the bills left a saving of 2 per cent, on £30,000, equal to £676 per annum.

This case is a type of many where a change in the method of financing has effected large savings, and relieved embarrassment.

owing to the firm, and should not permit any customer to extend the ordinary terms of credit unless such extension is contracted for at the time when the goods are sold. The growing tendency to relaxation of terms of credit is an evil that can only be counteracted by the utmost firmness on the part of established houses. A proportion only of the usual discount should be allowed where accounts are not remitted promptly, and where practicable the whole discount should be forfeited.

The terms of payment should be printed on all invoice and statement forms, and it should also be intimated that interest will be charged on overdue accounts (»»).

The profitable handling of financial matters depends very largely upon the care and vigilance of the cashier, or other person entrusted with the duty of passing accounts both to be received and paid, and the principal will do well to supervise this work. A rough test may, however, be placed upon the results year by year. The discount on purchases and the discount on sales accounts may be compared with those of previous years. From the amount of purchases made during the year it may be readily computed how much discount *ought* to have been obtained, after allowing for loss of discount in cases where bills are given. The discount p. n sales can only be compared by way of average, as there is so much irregularity in the modes of payment; one customer will remit prompt cash, another will give an acceptance and another will pay at half-time, and so on. Nevertheless, the average should be much the same year by year in a steady business.

While advocating the utmost vigilance in making use of all the advantages which custom and usage allow in financial matters, the author cannot too strongly deprecate the unfair means that are sometimes resorted to in order to extort more than is justly due. If on no higher ground than that honesty is the best policy, it should be remembered that a reputation for fair dealing is an invaluable aid to a buyer.

Jm) Interest cannot be legally claimed until after notice has been given that it 1 be charged, hence the necessity for such intimation.

CHAPTER VIII.

Wages.

The most rigid exactness and precision should be observed in controlling the payment of wages, which constitute one of the largest and most important items of expenditure in a manufacturing business. All requisite statistics and information, as well as security against fraud, may be obtained by judicious organisation, with even less clerical labour than is involved in many of the clumsy and unsatisfactory methods in use, which afford neither information or security.

Inter alia it is necessary to know:— (i.) The amount paid in each department, or for each class of work, during any given period. (ii.) That no amounts are charged by the cashier other than those actually paid. (iii.) That the *time* workers are paid only for actual time employed. (iv.) That the *piece* workers are paid only for actual work executed.

The following plan, which fulfils all the above requirements, has for years been in operation in many large manufacturing concerns with entirely satisfactory results:—

Pay Tickets.—The overlooker of each department is furnished with a book of pay tickets, each page being ruled and perforated so as to form ten tickets, (see page 243). Duplicate coloured sheets, not perforated, alternate with the perforated sheets and receive impressions from carbon paper. These books remain in the counting-house during the week, and are handed out to the several overlookers in time for them to write out the pay tickets for the workpeople under their supervision. The books are then collected and verified (») by a trustworthy person, other than the pay clerk, whom we may style the *Wages Superintendent,* and the duplicate pages are cast up and initialed by him in ink. The perforated pay tickets are torn out and handed back to the overlookers, who distribute them amongst the workpeople (0). The books containing the duplicates are sent into the counting-house, and from them the money is counted and made ready.

A cheque should, where convenient, be drawn for the exact amount required, thus avoiding the temptation to misappropriate any surplus.

(n) The verification may be done either before or after the wages are paid, and, if after, mistakes may be rectified on the succeeding pay day. (0) For greater secnrity, the Wages Superintendent may distribute the tickets personally or by depnty, and may require the workpeople to furnish the amount due to them before handing over the tickets.

Pay Tables and Boxes.—The pay clerk is provided with a table divided into small numbered squares, and the amounts due to the workpeople are counted and placed on the squares bearing the numbers by which they are respectively known. Small tin boxes with impressed numbers are sometimes used as receptacles for the money, and are arranged in order on the table. The employes present their numbered tickets at the pay table and receive cash in exchange for them.

Departmental Summary.—A summary (seepage 245) classifying the wages according to the amounts paid in each department, or subdepartment, is regularly written up by transcribing the weekly totals from books containing the pay ticket duplicates.

Test of Results of Labour.—The results of labour employed in each department may be tested by comparing the totals shewn by the wages summary with the record of work week by week.

Collusion.—In order to guard against fraud by collusion between overlookers and workpeople, the task of writing out the pay tickets should occasionally, without previous notice, be deputed to another person.

Workpeoples' Record.—The wages superintendent should keep a *Workpeoples' Record* containing the numbers, names and addresses of all employes, particulars of the terms upon which they are severally engaged, dates when engaged and when discharged, alterations in rates of pay, and any other useful information. The numbers and names of the workpeople may also be entered at the commencement of the pay ticket books. It will be found necessary, owing to the constant changes, to revise the Workpeoples' Record occasionally, the names being re-written and new numbers issued.

The Wages Superintendent while verifying the pay tickets should compare the weekly earnings with the Workpeoples' Record and inquire into any discrepancy.

Piece-Work Record.—Systematic records should be kept of all work done and *piece-work* wages should be compared therewith. These records are usually kept in books specially ruled for the purpose and should comprise the following particulars, viz: The description of work, quantities, dates when commenced and finished, rate of pay, and amount. A column should be provided where necessary for payments on account.

The overlooker opens a distinct page in his book for each person under his supervision. In some cases it is convenient to have a separate book for each employe and in others tickets are used. It is quite impossible, owing to the many varieties, to give specimen rulings, or even to lay down a comprehensive method of recording work done. The records should, however, be thorough and systematic, and should be so arranged that the returns for the cost books and also for the departmental accounts may when necessary be compiled from them.

Timeworkers.—The timeworkers' wages should be verified by the timekeeper's book.

Metallic Check System.—There is, perhaps, no more reliable check upon time workers than what is known as the metallic check system. Each employ6 is furnished daily with metallic discs bearing the number assigned to him or her. On entering the works the discs are dropped into a receptacle, and the numbers are afterwards marked off in the timekeeper's book (see specimen, page 244). Several ingenious contrivances have been invented for receiving the metallic discs, amongst which is a clock made to shift automatically, at set intervals, a receptacle with partitions; thus shewing late arrivals without the possibility of collusion.

It will be observed that the various functions connected with the computation, verification and payment of wages are performed by different parties, while they are so linked together that the successful perpetration of fraud involves the complicity of several persons.

FORM FOR PAY TICKET BOOK.

Each page of the book should form ten tickets. The alternate sheets for the duplicates should be of coloured paper, and need not be ruled.

The sides of the squares indicate four divisions of time during the day, *e.g.,* before Breakfast, after Breakfast, after Dinner, and overtime. Where there are only three divisions a triangle may be used and where only two a X-The half stroke signifies a late arrival or early departure and the figures (3o) mark the short time in minutes. No employe should be allowed to leave at an irregular time without a special permit.

FORM FOR WAGES BOOK.

The following form of Wages Book may be employed where the use of pay tickets is not convenient. The book is ruled to record the wages for thirteen pay days, without re-writing the names. A separate page or portion of a page is appropriated to each department. A Summary is prepared by transcribing the weekly totals of all departments to a page set apart for that purpose.

CHAPTER IX.

Mill Or Factory And Wareiiousr Books.

We are now to explore a region usually regarded by the skilled book-keeper as *terra incognita,* and where, moreover, he would esteem himself wholly as a trespasser.

Innovations in this direction, when prompted solely from a theoretical acquaintance with the science of book-keeping, are for the most part useless and are often mischievous, but there is no excuse for leaving a most important sphere of account-keeping to be framed and organised entirely by empirical ingenuity.

In many manufacturing concerns the mill books consist almost entirely of rough and ready records of the overlookers or heads of departments, who write down only what is absolutely essential for the purposes of their supervision, and not infrequently sturdily oppose any increase to this branch of their duties.

In any endeavour after reform the wise utilization of existing agencies will materially enhance the chances of success. Moreover, any system of mill books must, to a large extent, be organised out of the imperfect methods which necessity and accruing experience have brought into practice. The records of the overlookers may, if well arranged and made permanent, form a practical basis for a simple and perfect system.

As an outcome of these views, after very careful investigation into the essential requirements of the various departments of manufacture, the forms given on pages 262 to 271 have been drawn up, and with various modifications they are adopted by many first-class firms.

The stock and cost books hereinafter described may be kept by the overlookers or managers of departments, or, if secrecy is desired, may be written up in the counting-house from returns made by them. The prices and cost calculations may, if preferred, be entered in cipher.

The person who is responsible for the oversight of stock or *stores,* in any department is expected to satisfactorily account for all that he receives, and should at any time be able to furnish from his books, without surveying the articles, the exact quantity of any particular commodity in his keeping. Besides which, his accounts should be capable of verification by comparing the quantities on hand, shewn by the periodical stock-taking, with the surplus shewn by his books.

In order to guard against extravagance the storekeeper may be instructed to require the production of a ticket, signed by an overlooker and countersigned by a manager or other official, authorizing him to deliver out articles in his keeping. These tickets will constitute the storekeeper's vouchers for articles issued, and they should be occasionally compared with his books by an independent official. The cost of the tickets is small, and, if printed in suitable forms, they may be made out very readily.

In accounting for material, stock, or stores, regard must be had to *quantities* and not *values.* The introduction of values will only lead to hopeless confusion, and will serve no useful purpose.

When a larger quantity is withdrawn than is required for the immediate purpose, it should always be returned to the place of withdrawal, and should not be kept over until another opportunity occurs of using it.

In considering the various books *(p)* required, we shall commence with the purchase of materials, and advance step by step through the several stages of manufacture, concluding with the warehousing, consignment, and sale of the finished goods.

In the first place we must deal with the MILL BOOKS RELATING TO PURCHASES.

These differ essentially from the books connected with the several processes of manufacture.

The first book which comes to our notice is the ORDER BOOK.—A written order, signed by a principal, or authorized official, should be given for all goods purchased, and a copy of the order should be retained for reference. Order books containing duplicate forms are convenient for this purpose. The forms should be numbered consecutively, and should provide for conditions as to packing, carriage, date and place of delivery, terms of payment, instructions as to sending delivery notes and invoices, and any other material particulars. Reference should be made to sample where necessary, and the order should in all respects be carefully worded (see *Statute of Frauds,* page 295).

When the invoices come to hand they should be compared with the duplicate order forms, and may also be marked with the order number.

In every instance where it is necessary or desirable to supervise the receipt and disposal of articles purchased, the particulars thereof should be recorded in a *Stock and Cost Book.* The size and ruling of the book must be arranged so as to accommodate the particular characteristics of the articles to be recorded therein; but it will be *(p)* It will, of course, be understood that it is quite impossible to provide forms exactly suitable for every variety of business. The specimens are confined to the Woollen and Worsted trades, and in some instances merely general outlines are given, which may be modified to suit special requirements. The books required by the Bilk Spinner are very similar to those for Worsted Spinning.

observed that the same fundamental principles prevail throughout the several books hereafter described, viz.:— (i.) The articles RECEIVED are recorded in *quantities,* and the *cost price* is given. (ii.) The quantities ISSUED are shown, and their *destination* is indicated by means of reference numbers. (lii.) The *total quantity* ISSUED is made to agree with the *quantity* RECElVED.

Articles returned after being issued may be entered in red ink in the issued columns, and the quantities returned should be deducted when extending into the total issued column.

Form 1 is suitable for RAW MATERIAL PURCHASED.

Three entries are given as examples; the first is all issued to the Combing Department to be made into Tops (see Combing or Tops Stock and Cost Book, Form 7); of the second and third entries a portion of each is issued for making woollen yarn (see Woollen Yarn Making Stock and Cost Book, Form 6).

The Combing and Woollen Lot reference numbers to which the material is issued are indicated by the figures *above,* and the lbs. weight by the figures *beneath* the line, thus—TffVrs i."-..

When the whole of a parcel has been issued the lower figures are added laterally, and their sum is extended into the *Total lbs. issued* column.

Unless the material purchased is already scoured and dyed, it has to pass through one or both of these ptocesses before it is used in making yarn *(q).* The scouring causes a large reduction in weight, in some instances as much as 7o per cent., and a new calculation is therefore necessary.

Thus—the material in its raw state, 5lo lbs. cost 8fd. per lb. = 18: 11: 1oJ—the weight after scouring and dyeing is 19o lbs., therefore ijjJ1:10 = 1: 11i per lb.; to which add the price per lb.
for scouring and dyeing, say 2d., together making 2: i per lb.

The increased price and the reduced weight are entered in their respective columns, and the lbs. issued will of course correspond with the reduced weight. The percentage of reduction by scouring may be recorded for guidance in future buying.

When the material is sent out to dye it is well to provide extra columns for recording the dates sent and returned, the Dyer's name, artd the price.

(q) In making woollen yarn it is customary to scour the whole parcel of material, which may then be distributed into several lota. In combing lots, however, the whole parcel of wool is usually both scoured aud combed, and may be distributed into several spinning lots after combiDg. In the latter case, therefore, the reduction in scouring more conveniently falls into the calculation for the combing lot, and the unscoured weight is consequently entered as i«tued to the combing lot. Where quantities of various material are blended in anticipation of spinning, it may perhaps be desirable to keep a separate Blend Book.
This book may be apportioned *(r)* or separate books may be used, according to convenience, so that the various descriptions of material may be kept distinct.

FORM 2 is suitable for YARN PURCHASED in the hank, or bundle, or warp, and either dyed or undyed.
The first specimen entry represents a quantity of white worsted yarn, a portion of which is handed out to dye Shade No. 3o (see Yarn Shade Register, Form 12), and other portions are handed out in the white for weaving pieces Nos. , say, 1473o, 14876, 14895. These several portions exhaust the purchase, and the items afe added laterally and extended into the *Total lbs. issued* column.
The second specimen entry represents a quantity of coloured yarn purchased in the dyed state, which is at once issued to its respective Shade No., say, 171.

The book may be apportioned *(r)* for different classes of yarn and the ruling may be modified for special characteristics. Woollen, worsted, cotton, and silk yarn may be kept distinct from one another.
FORM 3 is suitable for YARN PURCHASED on the spool or bobbin, and may be combined with Form 2 if preferred. FORM 4 is suitable for DYEWARES, CHEMICALS, SOAP, OIL, &c.
The quantities of invoices when given in tons, cwts., &c, should be reduced to lbs., and the weights issued should be recorded in lbs.

When the material is handed out to different departments, initials indicating the department may be given above the quantity issued, in order to facilitate the departmental analysis.

The book may be apportioned for different classes of material, or separate books may be used *(r)*. FORM 5 is suitable for MILL FURNISHINGS AND LOOSE UTENSILS.

This is merely an outline form for articles purchased in bulk, to be handed out by the storekeeper as required *(e.g. . Belting, Strapping, Brushes, Baskets, Oil Cans, &c., &c.)* ln the classification of the invoices in the Purchases Day Book, these articles are entered under the column headed Mill Furnishings, &c., sub-head " *Store."* From this stock book the analysis for departments is prepared so far as regards the items in the *Store* column.

Having described the Stock and Cost Books for recording things purchased, let us now consider the MILL BOOKS relating to the PROCESSES OF MANUFACTURE.

To the right hand of Forms 6, 7, and 8 supplementary columns are added for abstracting the work done in the department, but they may (r) When a Stock Book is apportioned, the respective divisions may be indicated in the same way as the letters of an alphabetical index to a ledger.
be omitted where departmental accounts are not required. The amounts extended into these columns should be added up and carried forward from page to page.

The space allowed in the forms for the calculation of each lot must entirely depend upon the ordinary requirements of the particular business. ln some cases four or five lots may usually be calculated on one page, in others, where many different parcels of material are mixed in one lot, a whole page may be required.

Material which is put out to work in any of the processes may be entered up in exactly the same form as though the process had been carried on at home. The outworker's name, and the dates, handed out and returned, should be recorded.

FORM 6 is suitable for a WOOLLEN YARN MAKING STOCK AND COST BOOK.
The specimen entry represents a lot of black weft, part of which is handed out for weaving Piece No. 1457o (see Piece Making Book, Form 11.), the remainder is supposed to be in stock.

The stock reference numbers in the first column refer back to the entries in the Raw Material Stock and Cost Book, Form 1.

The price charged for scribbling, carding, and spinning represents the ordinary trade charge, and is calculated upon the weight of yarn *produced.*

When different thicknesses are spun from the same lot, columns may be provided for each size, as in the Worsted Yarn Making Stock and Cost Book, Form 8.

Where yarns are *twisted* or *doubled,* a new stock record and calculation of cost is required, and this may be made in a similar form to the yarn lot, or a distinct book may be kept for *Twists.* The stock reference numbers would refer to the yarn lots of which the Twist was composed.

FORM 7 is suitable for a COMBING (or TOPS) STOCK AND COST BOOK.
The specimen entry represents a combing lot, the tops from which are handed over to the Spinning Department (see Worsted Yarn Making Stock and Cost Book, Form 8), and form the material of Spinning Lot 85.

The stock reference number in the first column refers back to the entry in the Raw Material Stock and Cost Book, Form 1.

The price charged for combing represents the ordinary trade charge, and is calculated upon the weight of tops *produced.* The value of the *Noils* is deducted before the cost per lb. of tops is calculated.

The Noils are represented as partly sold, and the remainder as handed over to be spun in a Woollen Lot No., say, 161.

The tops produced which are here all issued to one spinning lot might be issued to several.

Where tops are purchased by the firm, the quantities purchased should be entered in Form i, a separate book or portion of a book being appropriated to them if desired.

FORM 8 is suitable for a WORSTED YARN MAKING STOCK AND COST BOOK.

The specimen entry represents a lot of worsted yarn made from Combing Lot 77, and portions of which are spun to two different counts or sizes. A part of the 2/48's yarn is issued to Shade No. 31 (see Yarn Shade Register, Form 12), and the remainder is supposed to be in stock.

The trade charge for roving and spinning differs with the counts or thickness of the yarn. The cost per lb. of the material, at the decreased weight after spinning, is first ascertained, and to this the trade charge for roving and spinning must be added to find the cost of each size of yarn. A slight allowance may be made for the difference in waste in spinning to the various sizes.

The headings of the columns for *counts* should not be printed but written in each case, and a sufficient number of columns should be provided for the average variety of counts spun from the same lot.

Warp, weft and *hank* may be marked above the lbs. produced, and the slight difference in price may be indicated as required.

Before proceeding to describe the Piece Cost Book, it is desirable that we should refer to several books which are almost entirely of a technical character, but which form connecting links between the Yarn and the Piece Cost Book.

In the manufacture of plain goods very many of the complicated details involved in making fancy goods are avoided, but provision is made for the most intricate case, and it is left to the discretion of the reader as to what he may conveniently omit in his own particular trade.

In smaller concerns certain books which are here kept separate may be combined; in other cases perhaps further subdivision may be desirable.

The head warehouseman is expected to furnish the mill manager with particulars of every order received by him. These particulars are entered in the PIECE ORDER BOOK at the MILL (see Form 9).

The number of pieces to be delivered in each month can be ascertained by adding up the figures in the respective month columns, and the manufacturer may thus guard against contracting to deliver more pieces than he can get ready in the given time.

With a view to avoid unnecessary changes of the loom gears all orders should be classified as they come in, according to the make of cloth. The basis of classification is usually the sley or reed. The orders received and the details of construction *(s)* of all pieces woven with a particular sley or reed are entered on the page or pages appropriated to them in the ORDERS MAKING CLASSIFICATION BOOK (see Form 1o).

The specimen entry sets out the details for construction of Piece No. 1457o (see Form 11).

An index to this book may be kept to indicate the folio where any range may be found.

When the pieces are delivered the entries in the Orders Received columns should be marked off.

After classification the next step is to ascertain and get ready the quantities of the various yarns required to fulfil orders, as to which the O. M. C. Book affords full information.

In preparing to make fancy goods, if the yarn is purchased in the white the required quantity of each shade must be handed out to dye; if coloured yarns are purchased then the necessary orders must be given to the spinner.

In order to control efficiently the storing of fancy yarns, which often number several hundred different shades and many different qualities and sizes, it is necessary to keep a YARN SHADE REGISTER (see Form 12).

In this register are recorded the quantities *required, ordered, received* and *issued.*

The quantity *required* is recorded so that a sufficient supply may be prepared in readiness for weaving the pieces on order (/).

The quantity *ordered* is recorded, as it is frequently desirable to order more than is required for immediate purposes. The date ordered is inserted for facility of reference, especially where coloured yarns are purchased from the spinner, who may, and often does, send more or less than is ordered.

Different counts and qualities of yarn should be kept in distinct portions of the register, and the qualities may be indicated by letters, thus—A12, B12, &c.

For indentification the box or receptacle containing the yarn, or the yarn itself, should be labelled with the quantity, stock and shade numbers, and the counts or skeins.

(a) A book should be kept for recording the particulars for construction of all goods offered for sale, the ranges being numbered consecutively, and the Orders Making Classification Book may be entered up therefrom. *(t)* The delivery of goods is frequently delayed becanse of the supply of a particular shade becoming exhansted.

As already explained, all yarn *purchased,* whether dyed or undyed, is *first* entered in the Yarn Stock and Cost Book, Form 2 or 3, and all yarn *made* is first entered in the Yarn Making Stock and Cost Book, Form 6 or 8. Each quantity *handed out* to weave is entered as *issued* from these Stock and Cost Books, and, if not woven in the white, is entered as *received* in the Yarn Shade Register. The reference numbers are inserted both in the Stock and Cost Book and Register.

Each quantity of dyed yarn handed out to weave *(u)* is entered in the Shade Register as *issued,* the piece reference number being inserted.

The specimen entry in Shade 3o relates to yarn *purchased* in the white (entered as issued from Form 2), and afterwards dyed to Shade 3o; 7J lbs. of this are issued to weave Piece 1457o (see Form 11).

The specimen entry in Shade 31 relates to yarn made on the premises (entered as issued from Form 8), and afterwards dyed to Shade 31; lbs. of this are also issued to weave Piece 1457o (see Form 11).

It must not be overlooked in comparing the stock on hand with the difference between the quantities *received* and *issued,* that the yarn gains in weight by the process of dyeing, and this gain must be inserted.

To find the cost price of any shade of yarn, refer back, by help of the Stock reference number, to the Stock and Cost Book, and add, where necessary, the cost of dyeing as indicated in the Shade Register, allowance being made for increase of weight in dyeing.

When the time arrives for the piece to be woven a WEAVER'S TICKET is prepared (see Form 13).

The particulars necessary for filling up this ticket are obtained from the O. M. C. Book, Form 1o. The ticket passes first into the hands of the warper and thence to the weaver, and is produced to the overlooker when the piece is woven. The overlooker in exchange hands the weaver a pay slip (see page 243) which authorises the cashier to pay the weaver wages for the work done.

As each piece is put into work the full details thereof are entered in the PIECE MAKING or BALK BOOK (Form 11).

A serial number is given to the piece, which it bears until it is delivered finished at the warehouse.

The folio of the O. M. C. Book (Form 1o) is inserted for reference, and from that book the details, including the weight of warp and weft, are obtained.

(u) In large concerns it is often convenient to keep a separate book in which to record the several quantities handed ont to weave, and the total issued from each shade is entered weekly in the Shade Register.

Except in the case of goods made for stock, the cost is calculated and orders are taken at prices fixed long before the pieces are put into work. It is, however, very essential for future guidance, as well as for checking purposes, that the *actual* cost should be calculated after the goods are made. It is not convenient to make these calculations in the Piece Making Book, as it would there be necessary to reckon the cost of each individual piece. A much more effective check, and one that involves much less labour, can be imposed by abstracting the necessary particulars of pieces of one particular make and including them in one calculation.

The PIECE COST BOOK (Form 14), may be utilised both for costing ranges and for checking the actual cost of the pieces after they are made.

The percentages for Pattern Making and Warehouse Expenses and General Charges, may be determined with the help of the Manufacturing Account, Sections I. and II. (see page 221), by the following method, viz.:—Compare the *aggregate value of work done* in those processes mentioned in the Piece Cost Book— (i.) With the aggregate cost of pattern making.
(ii.) With the aggregate of the warehouse expenses and general charges; and according to the proportions which these bear in the aggregate, so should be the ratio of charge in the individual calculations.

The percentage of profit must always be determined by the circumstances of the business.

According to this principle of costing goods the *non-manufacturing* charges are equally distributed over the *work done* in the Weaving and subsequent departments, and it is believed that this will be found the safest and most reliable method. The charges might be distributed on the basis of the *wages paid* in these departments, but to do so would require additional calculations. The basis of charge might also include the cost of material where the goods made are all of the same class, but where the material used in certain goods is more expensive than that used in others the charges would be unequally distributed.

We have now to consider the books required in the Warehouse. The particulars of each order received are recorded in the WAREHOUSE ORDER BOOK (Form 15).

The written orders should be carefully preserved and numbered consecutively. By the aid of this book the manager of the warehouse is able to keep in view the orders on hand from each customer, and to see that they are duly executed. A separate portion of the book is appropriated to each customer, and an alphabetical index is kept to indicate the customer's folio on the same principle as an ordinary ledger index.

The Yarn Spinner will find it necessary to keep an order book either at his mill or warehouse, or at both places, but the form of the book must entirely depend upon his particular class of trade. The form should provide *inter alia* for the following particulars, viz:— Date, consecutive number of order, description of yarn, mark, counts or skeins, price, terms, date for delivery, whether on spool or bobbin, or in hank or warp, quantity, and any special particulars. It should also provide for dates of delivery and quantities delivered.

It is sometimes convenient to keep the record of skeps in this book (see also page 229).

The WAREHOUSE STOCK BOOK (Form 16), is suitable for piece goods.

The distinctive numbers given to the pieces and recorded in the Piece Making Book, Form n, are utilised only for *manufacturing* purposes. The particulars of all pieces as they are delivered at the warehouse are entered in the Warehouse Stock Book in consecutive order, and a ticket, bearing the Warehouse Stock Book Serial No., is attached to each piece. The Warehouse No. is used for *selling* purposes, and is recorded in the Sales Day Book entry.

The Warehouse Stock Book should be periodically compared with the Piece Making Book (t), and at stocktaking every piece not on hand should be traced through the Sales Day Book as sold. Returned goods will, of course, be likewise traced through the Returns Sales Day Book.

The Yarn Spinner who keeps a stock of yarn at his warehouse may also require a Stock Book showing the quantities of each class of yarn received and sold, with references to the Sales Day Book, but the *Making* Stock and Cost Books (see Forms 6 and 8) may ordinarily be utilised for this purpose.

Goods consigned to Agents for sale should not be entered in the Sales Day Book until actually sold. The *quantities* forwarded to the agent should be recorded as each delivery is made in a CONSIGNMENT STOCK BOOK (see Forms 17 and 18).

When the Agent furnishes his Account Sales (usually at the end of each month), the quantities sold should be entered in the Sales Day Book and marked off in the Consignment Stock Book.

Goods returned by the Agent to the firm must be entered in the Quantities or Yards *Sold* columns in red ink.

Goods returned by customers to the Agent must be re-entered as a new consignment to the Agent.

At the date of stocktaking, and at other stated periods, the Agent should be required to furnish a list of stock in his hands, and the Consignment Stock Book should be verified therewith.

A separate portion of the book, or a separate book, should be appropriated to each Agent, and different classes of goods may also be kept distinct.

(v) For convenience of reference the Warehouse No. maybe inserted in the Piece Making Book.

It may be well here to recapitulate the various entries of material, in order that we may trace it through its several stages from the purchase to the completion of the manufacture and ultimate sale.

Raw Material Purchased is entered in the Raw Material Stock and Cost Book, Form 1.

Yarn Purchased, whether dyed or undyed, is entered in the Yarn Purchased Stock and Cost Books, Forms 2 and 3.

Raw Material made into Yarn is entered as issued from Form 1 and as *received* in either (i.) the Woollen Yarn Making Stock and Cost Book, Form 6, or (ii.) the Combing or Tops Stock and Cost Book. Form 7, and thence into the Worsted Yarn Making Stock and Cost Book, Form 8. If the Yarn is *twisted* it may also pass through the Twist lot.

The entries in the O. M. C. Book, Form 1o, may be disregarded in tracing the material.

Yarn handed out to weave is entered as issued from the Yarn Purchased, or Yarn Making, Stock and Cost Books, Forms 2 and 3, or 6 and 8.

If the yarn is plain the quantity both of warp and weft is entered direct from the Yarn Stock and Cost Books to the Piece Making Book, Form 11. If it is fancy yarn it passes first through the Yarn Shade Register and thence into the Piece Making Book.

An intermediate book, between the Yarn Shade Register and the Piece Making Book, may be employed to collect the quantities issued to weave, so that they may be entered in weekly totals in the Yarn Shade Register.

The pieces when *finished* are forwarded to the warehouse and there entered in the Warehouse Stock Book, Form 16, and when *sold* they are entered in the Sales Day Book.

It is, therefore, possible to follow all material from the raw to the finished state, and from the purchase to the sale. The various entries may, if desired, be afterwards called over from one book to another, and when this is done a theft or miscarriage of goods in any stage may be detected.

RECORDS OF WORK IN DEPARTMENTS.

It has already been stated (see page 22o) that in order to ascertain the profit or loss on the Manufacturing Departments it is necessary to keep a record of work done under each process.

Weekly returns should be made to the Counting house, and the requisite particulars may be obtained from the following sources:— (i.) Combing and Woollen and Worsted Spinning Departments.

The quantities of work done, and the trade charges therefor, in these departments may be abstracted from the Stock and Cost Books (see Forms 6, 7 and 8); the supplementary columns being added for this purpose.

(ii.) Winding, Warping and Sizing.

This work is in many cases paid for by the piece, and the quantities are consequently recorded for the purpose of calculating the wages: these records should be made in permanent form. Even where timeworkers are employed the quantities are necessarily weighed before being handed out to weave. There is, therefore, no difficulty in making returns of work done. Where the charges for Warping, Winding and Sizing are separately entered in the Piece Cost Book, Form 14, the prices may be obtained therefrom.

(iii.) Weaving Department.

In costing piece goods the processes of putting up and weaving are often charged at double the weaver's wages, and in such cases the value of work done is readily ascertained by doubling the aggregate of the weavers' wages. The charge for goods woven in fast looms is sometimes calculated at two and a half times the weaver's wages. Although this method of calculation is not universal the weaver's wages usually forms the basis of the charge.

(iv.) Scouring, Milling, Fulling, Dyeing, Finishing, Mending, &c.

Much of this work is paid for by the piece, and the quantities recorded for wages paying may be utilised. The number of pieces passing through the processes may, of course, be ascertained from the Piece Making Book. Where the charges for these processes are separately entered in the Piece Cost Book, Form 14, the prices may be obtained therefrom.

When the Dyer misses the shade required and has to re-dye the material, he must not charge twice for his work unless he would be entitled, in the circumstances, to a double charge if he were trading apart from the concern.

The price for dyeing coloured yarns is often averaged, excepting blacks and blues.

The overlookers may be supplied with forms, where necessary, on which they may record daily the quantities of material or yarn, or the number of pieces operated upon in their respective departments. These records may be handed in to the counting house weekly and may there be entered up in permanent form.

It is unnecessary to give outlines for these weekly returns, but they should be ruled and printed in order to save as much writing as possible, and to secure uniformity they should supply the following information, viz: Date, description of material, quantity, trade price, colour, description of work or process, and any further essential particulars.

A Summary of the Work Done in all Departments should be entered up in the counting-house, in the same form as the Summary of Wages (see page 245).

Any serious leakage will be promptly brought to light by comparing weekly the *work done* with the *wages paid* in each department.

In many large concerns a weekly or monthly summary is prepared, according to Form 19, with a view to shew roughly what is known as the" Machinery Profit " for the time being.

The amounts of wages and work done are obtained from the respective summaries.

The Material consumed can be readily ascertained in certain departments, but not in others (for instance, it is not practicable to take stock of dyewares at frequent intervals); consequently the material consumed must be omitted until stock is taken.

The Average of Standing Expenses is based upon the Departmental Accounts prepared in previous years.

The difference between the amounts in the columns headed *Total Cost* and *Trade charges for work done* represents either Profit or Loss.

A great desideratum amongst manufacturers is a simple method of approximating the result of their trading at brief intervals, and by this Summary the *machinery* or *manufacturing* profit is arrived at. The *selling* profit on goods sold for the time being may be abstracted from the Sales Day Book and Piece Cost Book.

STOCKTAKING.

Stocktaking is a very important feature in preparation for the Balance Sheet, and the greatest care should be observed in ascertaining and taking down quantities, in fixing prices, in calculating the items, and in casting up columns.

Very frequent errors find their way into balance sheets through the medium of the stock valuations, upon the correctness of which the financial books afford no check. All guessing at quantities and reckless estimates are greatly to be deprecated, since erroneous conclusions thus arrived at may entail very serious consequences.

Quantities should, as far as possible, be verified with the Stock and Cost Books.

Calculations and additions should be made by one person and examined by another.

Prices may be fixed in ordinary cases on the following principles:—

All goods purchased, such as *Raw Material, Yarns, Dyewares, Chemicals, Soap, Oil, Size, &c,* should be taken at cost price, plus carriage and any charges in connection with buying, such as brokerage, commission, &c. The usual discount allowed by the vendors should be deducted.

Goods in process of manufacture should be taken at the cost of the material, calculated on the above-mentioned basis, plus the usual trade (or country price) for the process or processes through which the goods have passed. *Manufactured Yarns and Tops* may be taken at cost book prices (see Forms 6, 7 and 8, pages 263—265), less discount on the material.

The fluctuations in market value of material and yarns should be taken into account only where positive gain or loss has resulted therefrom. In determining whether gain or loss has actually accrued, regard must be had to the orders on hand which have to be executed, and the prices at which they have been accepted. Market values, however, will seldom form a reliable basis, and, except in cases of speculation or extraordinary fluctuations, *cost* prices should be adopted.

Piece Goods, finished and on order, may be valued at selling prices, a percentage being allowed to provide against the following deductions *(w),* viz:— (i.) Interest for the term of credit. (ii.) The usual discount. (iii.) Possible claims, damages, shorts, &c. (iv.) The loss which may be incurred on goods returned. (v.) Agent's commission, Carriage (if not paid by customer), cost of packing and delivery, and any special charges. *(w)* To these deductions there might he added the average loss by Bad Debts. *Piece Goods, not on order,* may be classified as

(i.) Ordinary saleable stock,

(ii.) Job lots, and old and damaged stock.

In valuing these, allowance must be made not only for the deductions referred to above, but also for the following, viz:— (i.) Interest on the probable term that the goods will remain in stock. (ii.) Tendency to depreciate in value, (iii.) Warehouse and Office expenses. (iv.) Selling Expenses. (v.) Selling Profit.

It must be remembered that profit is not made until the sale has been effected. Many of the above mentioned deductions are frequently overlooked; and there is, in fact, a very general disposition to overvalue Piece Stock.

The safest and most effective method of valuation is to take down prices at which the goods can be sold without doubt, and then to allow a percentage sufficient to cover interest, expenses, deductions, and profit. This percentage should be the same at each stocktaking.

If preferred, *saleable* piece goods may be valued at cost price, calculated at the cost of the yarn plus the usual trade charges for the processes of manufacture (see Piece Cost Book, page 269), but the selling price is usually a more reliable basis.

Old and damaged stock of all kinds should be the subject of special reduction.

FORMS for MILL or FACTORY and WAREHOUSE BOOKS,

pages 263 to 271.

Form 2. YARN (Purchased) STOCK AND COST BOOK, suitable for Yarn purchased in the Hank.

Form 3. YARN (Purchased) STOCK AND COST BOOK, suitable for Yarn purchased on Spool or Bobbin.

Form 4. DYEWARES, CHEMICALS, SOAP, OIL, &c, STOCK AND COST BOOK. The price should include carriage and any charges in connection with buying, such as commission, brokerage, etc.

Form 5. MILL FURNISHINGS AND LOOSE UTENSILS (Outline) STOCK AND COST BOOK.

Form 6. WOOLLEN YARN MAKING STOCK AND COST BOOK.

Lot No. *fj*. Quality or Description *fifTM*.... The Reference Nos. In the ease of a Manufacturer will be either to the Twist Stock and Cost Book, Yarn Shade Register, or Piece Making Book, and in the case of a Spiuner to the folio of the Sales Day Book where the sale is recorded.

The Reference Nos., if the Nolls or Tops are sold, are to the Day Book folio where Manufacturer himself, to the Spiuning Lot No. the sale is recorded, if 1 The " Tops " Reference Nos. will be either to tho Combing Tx't or Bought Tops Stock Rook. t The "1ssued" Reference Nos. in the case of a Manufacturer will be either to the Shade Register or Piece Making Book, and in the case of a Spinner to tho Sales Day Book folio where the sale is recorded.

Four or more of these forms may be printed on each page. Peculiar Processes of Finishing may be stated separately.

Form 19. SUMMARY shewing Machinery or Manufacturing Profit on WORK DONE in DEPARTMENTS.

APPENDIX.

I. Alphabetical Index To Ledger: Vowel System. II. Different Methods Of Preparing A Trial Balance. III. Interest Calculations. IV. How To Discover And Avoid Common Errors.

V. The Advantages Of A Professional Audit.

VI. Income Tax. VII. Bills Of Exchange, Promissory Notes, Cheques, &c. VIII. Information On Mercantile Subjects.

APPENDIX.

I. Alphabetical Index to Ledger: Vowel System.

The principle of this index, which is now very generally adopted where accounts are numerous, is at once ingenious and simple, and effects a great saving of time as compared with the old method.

The space allowed to each letter of the usual alphabetical index is divided into six parts, each part being headed by one of the vowels *A E I 0 U or Y*. The name of the account is inserted in that

The horizontal spaces A, B, C and D, each represent one folio of the Alphabetical Index; the six vertical divisions represent the several spaces allowed on each folio for the vowels.

division which is headed by the *first vowel appearing in the name after the initial letter.* Thus, Barber, C. J. is entered under the vowel A division of the letter B; Dyson, Alfred is entered under the Y division of the letter D, and so on. The same plan may be adopted where the index to the Ledger is classified under *Towns*.

To find the folio of an account, open the alphabetical index at the initial letter of the title of the account, and then look down the column headed by the first vowel in that title.

In order to avoid the risk of opening two accounts for the same name the folio of the account should be indexed before writing the heading in the Ledger, and accounts capable of bearing two denominations should be indexed twice.

II. Different Methods of Preparing a Trial Balance.

The methods of balancing in use are numerous, but, allowing for modifications to accommodate the varying requirements of different branches of trade, the leading features of all the systems worthy of notice may be summed up as follows—

A Trial Balance may be prepared:—
(i.) By making a list of all Ledger accounts and placing alongside the name of each, in one column the sum of the postings to the Dr. side during the period and in another column the sum of the postings to the Cr. side. If the grand totals of both columns agree one with the other the books balance (see page 14). This method is practically incorporated in the system described in this treatise.

(ii.) By abstracting from the Ledgers a list of the Dr. and Cr. balances which remain after deducting the postings on the Dr. from those on the Cr. side of each account, or *vice versa*. The grand total of the Dr. balances should agree with the grand total of the Cr. balances.

(iii.) By preparing a detailed analysis of the Ledgers wherein all the postings are dissected, classified and reconciled respectively with the separate books oi entry. The analysis is made on paper ruled with four or five vertical money columns for each side of the Ledger; the several columus being headed to correspond with the books of entry. (iv.) By balancing each Ledger separately, thus:—

A. Ascertain the total of the balances of the particular

Ledger at the commencement of the period.

B. Ascertain from the separate books of entry the total of the postings made to either side of the Ledger during the period.

c. Ascertain the total of remaining balances at the end of the period.

Arrange as follows:— SALES LEDGER.

Dr. Commencing Dr. Balances, Jan. 1st 5000 o o

Postings from Sales Day Book... 1oooo o o

Postings from right-hand side of Cash Book 25 6 2

Transfers 1o o o 15o35 6 2

Cr. Postings from left-hand side of Cash Book, including discount... 65oo o o

Postings from Returns Book 32o o o

Postings from Bills Receivable Ledger 3ooo o o

Transfers 1o o o

Balances remaining June 3oth 52o5 6 2

This method requires the entries in the separate books to be arranged so that the items posted to the different Ledgers may be readily dissected.

(v.) By the method explained in Sets

I. and II., which will be found to combine all the advantages obtained from the methods i. to iv.

In a small business where the books are kept by the proprietor himself, method ii. is perhaps the simplest and most appropriate. Methods i., iii. and iv. may be adopted with advantage in some instances, but method v. is recommended for ordinary cases.

Most works on book-keeping advocate the systematic arrangement of transactions in separate books of entry, but this seldom has for its object facility in balancing. The tendency is always towards arrangement according to the nature cf the entries, and the present treatise also takes full advantage of such classification. It, however, goes further, and requires the classification of the entries according to the Ledgers to which they are posted, in order that the total entries may be compared with the total postings in each Ledger.

III. Interest Calculations.

The method of calculating interest, for any number of days, or on Account Current, which is illustrated on the following page, is perhaps the best and simplest that has been designed.

The ruling of the page containing the account may of course be modified as required, and with the addition of other money columns varying rates of interest may be conveniently worked out on this plan.

The interest should be calculated on the nearest pound.

The rule on which the calculation is based is described in several works of Arithmetic, and is as follows:— *Multiply the principal by the number of days, and by double the rate per cent., and divide by* 73,000.

In the example the several balances are each multiplied by the number of days that they respectively rest until altered by another transaction. However, instead of completing the calculation of each item separately, the products are added up at the date when the interest is to be charged, and the *total* is multiplied by *double the rate per cent, and divided by* 73,000.

When the interest is 5 per cent., adding a cipher is equivalent to multiplying by double the rate. The division of 73,000 is effected by adding to the dividend one-third of itself, then one tenth of that third, and again one-tenth of the last quotient, and striking off 5 decimal places thus:— 183694 X double 5% or 1o... 1836940 add t/3rd... 612313 add i/toth... 61231 add i/toth... 6123.

This method, although sufficiently correct for all practical purposes, slightly overcalculates the interest, and to be exact, Jd. must be deducted for every £1o of interest. Therefore the interest in this case should be "25: 3: 3; fth of one penny being deducted.

If the balances are not always on the same side an additional column should be provided for extending the calculations on the Dr. aQd Cr. balances separately.

IV. How to Discover and Avoid Common Errors.

The preparation of a Trial Balance discovers only certain classes of errors; and balancing should be regarded as a means of proving the arithmetical accuracy of the postings, rather than as a means of discovering inaccuracies in the book-keeping. Prevention, in regard to errors, is obviously better than cure, and every reasonable precaution should be taken to ensure correct work as the book-keeping proceeds. Practice and experience are better than precept in this matter, but the following rules and suggestions will be found useful.

To prevent and avoid errors:— Call over all postings to the ledgers: where two or more clerks are employed, one clerk should take the book of entry and another the ledger.

Check all additions and the totals carried forward to subsequent folios. Ascertain also that the totals are carried forward to their proper columns.

Clear up and rule off Ledger Accounts as settlements are made, and always see that the remaining balance of an account is made up of current specific items.

Balance cash, and call over the items of the Banker's Pass Book and reconcile with the Cash Book, at frequent intervals. Irregularities in the cash, if honest, generally mean mistakes in the books.

Do not make erasures in the books.

Let each day's transactions be entered up during the day. The memory fails and omissions and mistakes arise when work is allowed to accumulate.

Always date entries and postings precisely—giving the year where not already stated—and keep them in order of date. Avoid interpositions at irregular dates.

Do not make indistinct figures, especially such as 0 and 6, 3 and 5, 7 and 9, which are often mistaken one for another.

Be careful to place the units, tens, hundreds, &c., directly under one another, as irregularity in this respect frequently causes errors in addition.

Never copy or transcribe figures that are added up without w-casting the copy.

To discover errors when preparing the Trial Balance; observe that:—

A difference of 1o/-may arise:— (i.) From an error in addition,—the pence and shillings columns should be re-cast. (ii.) From an error in posting,—call back and tick, *from the ledger to the books of entry,* one half the postings, *i. e.,* either those *with,* or those *without* double figures in the shillings column. If the mistake is not discovered whilst calling over the postings, the item which causes the error will be found without a tick in the books of entry.

Differences of £1o, £1oo, and /"1ooo usually arise from errors in addition. Such errors and also errors of 1o/-and iod., may be caused by the figure 7 or 9 being made so long that it comes before a figure or figures on the line beneath.

Errors of transposition are very common, such as 19s. 9d. for *fig: gs.* : od. , or 24: 5s.: od. for /2o: 4s.: 5d. The clerk who calls out the entries should habituate himself to careful articulation. It is not sufficient for him to say *nineteen nine* or *twenty, four, five,* but nineteen pounds, nine shillings, and twenty pounds, four shillings and fivepence. The posting clerk should repeat the figures.

Errors of transposition are very difficult to discover, but it can be ascertained at once whether a transposition is the cause of a difference in the trial balance by. adding as follows to the amount of the difference:—

To the pence, sufficient to make up a shilling:

To the shillings, sufficient to make the shillings as many as the number added to the pence:

To the pounds, sufficient to make the units of pounds as many as the number added to the shillings, and so on.

Thus, assume the difference in the trial balance to be.. 77 o 6

Add () 856 8j_6_o showing that a transposition of "85: 6: o for £8 : 5: 6 may account for the difference of £77: o: 6.

If the figures do not coincide as shewn, the difference in the Trial Balance is not the result of a single transposition of figures.

Sometimes an item is posted to the wrong side of the Ledger, in which case the columns of the Test Journal, when compared with the Balance Book, would show a difference of a like sum on both sides of the Ledger in question, and the item could be discovered by seeking for the amount in the book of entry.

When the abstracts of entries in the Test Journal exceed the abstracts of postings in the Balance Book, the difference may arise from an entry not being posted.

When the postings in the Balance Book exceed the entries in the Test Journal the error may arise from a posting being abstracted which belongs to a previous quarter. To prevent this a tick should be placed after the postings when the abstracts are made so as to show to what point the account has been abstracted. (See page 2o9).

Always persevere until a mistake is discovered; it will not rectify itself by delay.

V. The Advantages of a Professional Audit.

Amongst the many advantages of a professional audit, the following may be mentioned:—

The work of the book-keeper and cashier is thoroughly supervised; dishonesty is to a large extent prevented; and a tendency to relaxation of moral rectitude is corrected by the fear of detection which must always exist where an auditor is employed.

The books may be made to appear as though they were properly balanced by an unscrupulous or indolent book-keeper, for which reason the balancing should either be performed by, or checked and verified by, an Auditor. (x 6 is added to make up the peuoe to a shilling. 6 is added to the shillings to make them into 6, equal to the number added to the pence. 8 is added to the pounds to make the units 6, equal to the number added to the shillings.

The tens of the pounds require nothing further to be added to make them into 8, equal to the number added to the units.

A competent Accountant, who has a considerable practice, is always able to afford very useful information regarding the customary rates of profit, cost and expenditure, as well as depreciation. He can also direct attention to the weak points of a business and suggest remedies. Traders will therefore act wisely in obtaining the services of an experienced Accountant whose practice is principally amongst those who carry on their own particular business.

Partnership books should always be adjusted by an Accountant, if for no other reason than that he will act impartially and thus avoid disputes and suspicion. He will also be more likely to comply fully with the terms of the partnership deed, if any.

The books of a public company, or other enterprise where many are interested in the results, sliould also be audited by an Accountant. A false economy sometimes leaves this important office to parties interested in the undertaking, and who have no special qualification for the work. The author has brought to light many lamentable muddles in the affairs of public companies, which would have been avoided by the employment of a skilled Auditor.

An Auditor will be able to suggest improvements in the system of book-keeping, and in the conduct of the financial operations. He will also be able to advise as to the adjustment of revenue and capital items.

Accounts signed by a professional Auditor are usually accepted by Income Tax surveyors.

Although in the sets of books given in this treatise general plans have been laid down which can be adopted in every instance, there are many modifications of great utility which could be suggested by an Accountant conversant with the ever-varying requirements of different classes of business.

Principals and chief cashiers are strongly recommended to examine and verify the daily entries of cash received and paid. This ordinary act of business diligence may be performed in such a manner as not to offend the most sensitive, while the supervision of the "master's eye" may do much to prevent dishonesty. It will also check irregularities which cannot be detected by an Auditor, whose attendance is rare.

VI. INCOME TAX.

The mode of ascertaining profit for Income Tax Assessment differs very materially from the ordinary method of computing the profits of trade, and the points of difference are indicated in the following remarks.

The chief reason for the difference is that the duty is charged at the source whence the income arises, and the provisions of the enactments enable those who pay the tax to recover subsequently from the persons who are in the enjoyment of the income.

There are five schedules under which the Tax is charged:— *Schedule A.*—Touches income from Landed Property, including houses. The rack rent is the measure of charge, and in the absence of a rack rent, then the poor rate is the usual basis of assessment *(y)*. *Schedule B.*—Touches income derived from the use of land, as in farms, nurseries, market gardens, hop gardens, &c. The basis of assessment *(y)* is one half the real or annual value in England, and one-third in Scotland and Ireland. The farmer may now choose to be assessed under Schedule D in preference to Schedule

B.

The occupier pays the tax *(z)* under both Schedules A and B, and, if a tenant, he subsequently deducts the tax under Schedule A from the next payment of rent to his landlord.

Schedule C.—Touches income from Dividends of Public Funds, and the tax is deducted from the dividends when paid. *Schedule E.*—Touches income of persons in the employment of the State, Corporations and public bodies. *Schedule D.*—The most interesting to the Manufacturer, touches income from Trade, Manufacture, Profession, Employment or Vocation and any income not included in the other schedules. The assessment is based upon a return of income required, by notice, from the taxpayer. Much of the information necessary in preparing accounts for the return may be obtained from the printed rules and regulations on the form annexed to the notice.

The duty on *Professions, Trades, Employments or Vocations* is charged on the average profits for the *three years* preceding the year of assessment (a).

The duty on *Quarries, Ironworks, Gasworks, Waterworks, Canals, Railways, Tolls of Fairs, Markets,* and other concerns of a like nature is charged on the profit of the *preceding year.*

The duty on *Mines* is charged on the average profits of the *five years* preceding the year of assessment, but relief is granted when the mine fails, either wholly or partially.

If any of the above sources of income under Schedule D have commenced within the respective terms which form the basis of assessment, the profit is averaged from the period of commencing.

In estimating profits under *Schedule D. DEDUCTIONS ARE ALLOWED*— (i.) For Repairs to Premises occupied for the purpose of trade, (capital expended in improvements to premises is not allowed, see below).

(y) Assessment under Schedules A and B is made triennially. Under the Customs and Inland Revenue Act (Finance Act), 1894, a deduction of one-eighth of the gross rental is allowed in respect of lands (inolusive of Farm Houses and Buildings) and of one-sixth in respect of houses. (z) In the case of dwelling houses less than £10 per annum in value, or of houses let in tenements, or land let at a less period than one year, the tax is levied on the owner. (a) Profits made abroad are chargeable if the party receiving them resides in the United Kingdom. (ii.) For the Supply or Repairs of Implements, Utensils, or articles employed, not exceeding the average sum usually expended. (iii.) For Depreciation of Plant or Machinery—(as to other items of depreciation, see below). A fixed rate at which depreciation is to be calculated is usually determined by the Commissioners of the district, and this rate is adhered to at all appeals, notwithstanding that more or less may have been charged by the appellant. (iv.) For any Average Loss not exceeding the actual amount of loss after adjustment *(e.g.,* under a contract of insurance). (v.) For the Rent or Value of any Dwelling House or

Domestic Offices used for the purpose of any trade or profession, such sum not exceeding two-thirds of such rent or value as the Commissioners shall allow. (vi.) For Bad Debts; the net loss—Doubtful Debts may be estimated. A trade embezzlement is not allowed as a deduction. (vii.) lf a business is carried on in premises belonging to the firm the Assessment under Shedule A may be deducted. *NO DEDUCTIONS ARE ALLOWED*— (i.) For loss not connected with, or arising out of Trade, &c., or on account of capital withdrawn therefrom, or for any sum employed, or intended to be employed therein. (ii.) For capital employed in Improvement of Trade Premises. (As to Repairs, see above). (iii.) For Depreciation of Buildings, Premises, or Leases. (As to Plant and Machinery, see above). (iv.) For Interest on Capital *(b)* employed in the Trade or for any Annual Interest, Annuity, or other Annual Payment, payable out of profits. (v.) For Royalties (6). (vi.) For any sum recoverable under an Insurance or Contract of Indemnity. (vii.) For any Disbursements which shall not be money wholly and exclusively laid out for Trade, &c., or any disbursements or expenses of maintenance of parties, their families, or establishments, or any other domestic or private purposes, distinct from the purposes of Trade; in other words, for Principals' Salaries and Private Drawings. (viii.) For any sum paid as Income Tax on profits of any concern. *(b)* Interest paid to Bankers for the Trade account is allowed, as the Banker pays the tax. Income Tax should be deducted from Interest on borrowed money, Annuities, Royalties, &c, before paying same to the parties entitled thereto. (ix.) For Exhaustion of Minerals, sums expended in Pit Sinking. (x.) For premiums paid for Leases.

No direct power is given in the Income Tax Acts to compel the *production of books* and accounts in verification of the return. A surcharge may however be made, and if the taxpayer objects he can only appeal, and support his appeal by accounts.

EXEMPTION OR ABATEMENT—

Total exemption may be claimed on incomes not exceeding £16o.

Abatement of *£16o* is allowed on incomes not exceeding 4oo not entitled to exemption.

Abatement of *£1oo* is allowed on incomes over £4oo, but not exceeding £5oo.

Abatement is also allowed of the amount paid in respect of Life Insurance on life of Taxpayer or his wife (including Accidental Policies for death), to an extent not exceeding one-sixth of the total income. Any reduction however in respect of Insurance premiums has not the effect of giving exemption or abatement when the total income is thereby reduced so as not to exceed the prescribed limits of *£16o,* £4oo and 5oo respectively.

Income or profits of a married woman living with her husband are deemed by the Income Tax Acts to be her husband's profits, notwithstanding any settlement or the provisions of the Married Woman's Property Act of 1882. But where the wife's income is derived from any profession, employment, vocation or office, exemption or abatement may be claimed by both husband and wife, if the joint incomes do not exceed £500 (under Schedules D and E).

When the total income from all sources does not exceed the prescribed limits of £'160, £400 and 500 respectively, exemption or abatement is given in respect of duties payable (either by *deduction* as in Schedule C. or otherwise), under all the five schedules.

Partners, Joint Tenants, &c., may claim separate assessment in order to obtain exemption when their share of income is less than the prescribed limit. *EXEMPTION IS ALSO GRANTED*— (i.) To Charities, viz:—the income from property held on trust for charitable purposes, including rents and profits from land and houses under Schedule A, stock or dividends under Schedule C, and yearly interest and other annual payments under Schedule D. (ii.) To Hospitals, Public Schools, and Almhouses, viz:— The public buildings, and the income from land and houses belonging to them. (iii.) Friendly Societies and Industrial and Provident Societies, viz:— The stock, dividends, and interest belonging to them, under Schedule C; and the interest, and other profit and gains under Schedule. D. (it.) The Public Buildings and Halls in the Universities, the buildings of Literary and Scientific Institutions, &o. *REPAYMENT* may be obtained when the profits during the year of assessment turn out to be less than the average for the three years preceding the year of assessment. Notice must be given promptly. *APPEALS*—

Any person aggrieved by an assessment or surcharge is entitled to appeal, and notice of the place and time of hearing is given on the notice of assessment. Appellants are required to give ten days' notice, and three days before the day of appeal to transmit to the Surveyor of Taxes a complete account of profits for the term prescribed by the Act, giving particulars of all deductions. Assessments may not be altered before the time for hearing, except in cases specially authorised. A Chartered Accountant should be consulted in all cases of appeal.

As Schedule A Assessments are based upon the gross Poor Rate assessments, where it is sought to reduce the former below the latter, the Poor Rate assessment should first be appealed against. As to reducing the Poor Rate, the mode of assessment is not the same in different districts, and it is well to consult a first-rate local Valuer before appealing.

In order to avoid exposure to the general commissioners, who may be competitors in the same line of business, appeals may be made to Special Commissioners, if desired.

VII. BILLS OF EXCHANGE, PROMISSORY NOTES, CHEQUES, &c.

"Bills of Exchange were first introduced as a means of paying debts at distant places without the expense and risk of transporting the precious metals. Their use was afterwards greatly extended from another motive."

"It is usual in every trade to give a certain length of credit for goods bought. A dealer who has sold goods, for which he is to be paid in six months, but who desires to receive payment sooner, draws a bill on his debtor payable in six months and gets the bill discounted by a banker or other money lender, that is, transfers the bill to him, receiving the amount minus interest for the time it has still to run. It has become one of the chief functions of Bills of Exchange to serve as a means by which a debt due from one person can thus be made available for obtaining credit from another" *(c)*.

The acceptance of a bill fixes definitely the amount owing and the date of payment, and gives a more speedy legal remedy than in the case of an ordinary debt.

Bills of Exchange are either *Inland* or *Foreign*. An Inland Bill is one which is drawn and payable within the British Islands. Any other bill is a Foreign Bill.
(c) J. S. Mill.

The following are specimens of Bills and Promissory Note:—

Inland Bill.
No. iooi.
£250: 6: 5 Huddersfield, January 1st, 1885.

Four months after date pay to my order the sum of Two hundred and fifty pounds, six shillings and five pence, for value received.
ABRAHAM CROSLAND.
To Messrs. Brown, Jones & Co.,
Cheapside,
London.

When the bill is accepted, the following words are written across the face of it vertically:— "Accepted payable at the London & Westminster Bank.
Brown, Jones Co."
Foreign Bill.
No. 1oo2.
£470 : 1o: o New York, January 1st, 1885. (first,)

Forty days after sight of this our-i second, V of ,, secondland third,) r,,, (or third »

Exchange, first and third, of the same tenor and date unpaid, pay 0 (or first and second,) to the order of Messrs. Armitage, Sykes & Co. the sum of Four hundred and seventy pounds and ten shillings sterling, value received, and pass same to account, as advised by SCARBOROUGH & Co.

To Messrs. Eli B. Gough & Co.,
Huddersfield.

On arrival, this bill would be presented to Eli B. Gough A Co. for acceptance; the form of acceptance being similar to that given above. The date should, however, be added in this case, as the forty days date after sight, see Acceptance, page '288.

Promissory Note.
No. 1o3o.
52o: 16: o London, January 1st, 1885.

Three months after date, l *(d)* promise to pay to the order of Messrs. Robinson, Grey & Co. the sum of Five hundred and twenty pounds, sixteen shillings, value received.
WALTER GIBSON.
Payable at London and County Bank,
London.

(d) Or " we jointly and severally promise to pay," if more than one maker.

Bills or notes may be made payable by instalments.

The Bills of Exchange Act, 1882, codifies the law relating to Bills of Exchange, Cheques, and Promissory Notes, and applies to the whole of the

United Kingdom. The law is now the same for England, Ireland and Scotland, with one exception, which preserves to Scotland the rule as to the operation of a bill as an assignment of funds in the hands of the drawee.

Where a bill drawn in one country is negotiated, accepted, or payable in another, the rights, duties and liabilities of the parties thereto, so far as regards each distinct contract on the bill, are determined by the law of the place where the contract is made.

Definitions.

A BILL OF EXCHANGE is an unconditional order in writing, addressed by one person to another, signed by the person giving it, requiring the person to whom it is addressed to pay on demand, or at a fixed or determinable future time, a sum *certain* in money to, or to the order of, a specified person. The person who gives the order is called the *Drawer*; the person ordered to pay is called the *Drawee,* and the person to whom or to whose order the money is payable is called the *Payee.*

A PROMISSORY NOTE is an unconditional promise in writing made by one person to another, signed by the maker, engaging to pay, on demand or at a fixed or determinable future time, a sum certain in money to, or to the order of, a specified person, or to bearer.

A Promissory Note may be made by two or more makers, and they may be liable thereon jointly and severally according to its tenor.

Incompleteness, Irregularity and Alterations.

A bill is not invalid by reason that it is not dated, that it is antedated or postdated, or that it bears date on a Sunday, or that it does not specify the value given or that any value has been given therefor, or that it does not specify the place where it is drawn or the place where it is payable. Where a bill expressed to be payable at a fixed period after date is issued undated, or where the acceptance of a bill payable at a fixed period after sight is undated, any holder may insert therein the true date of issue or acceptance.

Where a bill or acceptance is materially altered without the assent of all parties liable, the bill is discharged, except as against a party who has himself made, authorized or assented to the alteration and subsequent indorsers.

The following alterations are *material,* namely, any alteration of the date, the sum payable, the time of payment, the place of payment, and the addition of a place of payment without the acceptor's consent.

A bill which has been altered need not necessarily be redrawn, provided the alteration is initialed by all the parties to the bill.

Negotiation and Indorsement.

When the holder of a bill payable to his order wishes to obtain or use the money before the bill becomes due, he indorses it by writing his signature across the back, thus rendering himself responsible for its due payment. The bill may then be negotiated, that is, transferred to another person in such a manner as to constitute the transferee the holder of the bill. A bill payable to Bearer is negotiated by delivery, but if payable to Order it must also be indorsed.

A bill may be indorsed *generally* by merely signing it in blank, when it becomes payable to Bearer, or *specially* by adding the name of a person to whom or to whose order it is to be payable.

When a bill contains words prohibiting transfer or indicating an intention that it should not be transferable, it is valid between the parties thereto, but is not negotiable. A bill may be made *not* negotiable by drawing it in the form, " pay John Brown only."

The drawer of a bill or any indorser may insert therein an express stipulation negativing or limiting his own liability to the holder, as by the addition of the words "without recourse to C D." A person who transfers a bill to another without indorsement is not liable thereon.

Where a person signs a bill otherwise than as drawer or acceptor, he thereby incurs the liability of an indorser to a holder in due course.

Acceptance.

The majority of those who read this work will have to do chiefly with Inland Bills, which when drawn are usually forwarded through the post or otherwise to the drawee for him to accept and return. Perhaps all that such readers will require is to know that the acceptance must be written on the bill and signed by the drawee, which may be done either before or after the drawer has signed. The mere signature of the drawee without additional words is sufficient.

Foreign Bills are usually payable at a specified period after sight. They are, as a rule, either sent by the drawer to the payee, or are sold by the drawer to another party, who transmits them to a creditor of his own, and he arranges for presentment for acceptance and payment. Such bills must be presented to the drawee for acceptance immediately they are received by the payee, in order to fix the maturity of the instrument. The acceptor should mark the date of his acceptance on the bill.

An agent to whom a bill is sent for negotiation should present it for acceptance at once, or he may be made personally liable.

Where a bill expressly states that it shall be presented for acceptance, or where a bill is drawn payable elsewhere than at the residence or place of business of the drawee, it must be presented for acceptance before it can be presented for payment.

When a bill is duly presented for acceptance, and is not accepted within the customary time (usually 24 hours), the person presenting it must treat it as dishonoured by non-acceptance. If he do not, the holder loses his right of recourse against the drawer and indorsers («).

(«) A ticket is usually attached to bills presented for acceptance, with the words

"Left for acceptance by of,

January 2nd, 1884," and, if the bill anthorizes, the words " To be accepted payable at London" may be added.

Acceptance supra protest, or *Acceptance for Honour,* is an acceptance by a party not liable on the bill, with the consent of the holder, to preserve the honour of the drawer or indorser. The bill must be protested against the drawee for non-acceptance before it is accepted *supra protest*. The acceptor for honour by accepting it engages that he will, on due presentment, pay the bill if it is not paid by the drawee. The bill must be duly presented to the drawee and protested for nonpayment before it is presented for payment to the acceptor for honour (see also Payment for Honour).

In some trades when an account becomes due it is customary for the creditor to pass a draft through his bankers for the amount, and to advise his debtor that he has done so. The draft in this case is practically presented for acceptance and payment at the same time.

Presentment for Payment.

Where a bill is payable on demand presentment must be made within a reasonable time. In determining what is a reasonable time, regard must be had to the nature of the bill, usage of trade, &c. A safe rule to follow is for presentment to be made on the day after the bill is received. Where a bill is not payable on demand, it must be presented on the day it falls due.

If a bill be *not duly presented for payment* the drawer and indorsers are *discharged* from liability. The bill must be presented on the exact due date, and neither before or after. Where a bill is not payable on demand the due date is determined as follows:—Three days, called *days of grace* are added to the time of payment as fixed by the bill, and the bill falls due on the last day of grace. Provided that when the last day of grace falls on Sunday, Christmas Day, Good Friday, or an authorized fast or thanksgiving day, the bill is due on the *preceding* business day. When the last day of grace is a Bank Holiday (other than Christmas Day or Good Friday), or when the last day of grace is a Sunday and the second day of grace a Bank Holiday, the bill is due on the *succeeding* business day.

There are no days of grace on bills drawn on Germany, France, Italy, Denmark, Sweden and Norway. In Russia there are ten days of grace on accepted bills.

Where no place of payment is specified, the bill is to be presented at the address, or last known address, of the drawee or acceptor.

Much trouble and difficulty may be avoided by passing all bills through the firm's bank.

Notice of Dishonour.

When a bill is dishonoured, notice of dishonour must be given to the drawer and each indorser, otherwise they will be discharged from liability.

A holder should give notice to parties living in the same place as himself in time to reach them on the day after the dishonour, and to parties living in a different place the notice should be sent off not later than the day after the dishonour. Although notice by the holder inures to the benefit of antecedent parties, they must not rely upon him giving notice to all who are responsible on the bill, as the holder is only bound to give notice to the party against whom he wishes to have recourse. Each indorser has the same period of time for giving notice, after receiving notice himself, as the holder has after the dishonour. Notice may safely be given in the following forms:— *Notice of Dishonour to Drawer.*—

Date and Address.

Please take notice that a Bill for £ drawn by you under date the on, and payable has been dishonoured by non-payment.

(Signed) C. D.

To A. B.

Notice of Dishonour to Indorser.—
Date and Address.

Please take notice that a bill for £ drawn by under date the on, and payable and which bears your indorsement, has been dishonoured by non-payment.

(Signed) A. B.

To Messrs. C. D. & Co.

Noting and Protest.

Although the expenses of noting can be recovered, noting is not necessary in the case of Inland Bills. Foreign Bills must be duly protested when dishonoured.

Payment *(f)* and Rights of the Holder.

Possession of the bill should be obtained by the party who pays it, and when a bill is taken up by an indorser after dishonour he should be careful to ascertain that the holder has duly preserved his rights of recourse.

When a bill is dishonoured by non-payment a holder may immediately sue on the bill in his own name, may enforce payment against all prior parties liable thereon, and no personal defence will be heard, as against a *holder in due course.*

The drawer who has been compelled to pay the bill may recover from the acceptor, and an indorser who has been compelled to pay may recover from the acceptor, or from the drawer, or from a prior indorser.

(f) Bills are more readily negotiated when made payable at a London Bank, and it ia usual therefore with oountry firms to insert the name of their Bank's London Agency. A bill accepted payable at the Acceptor's Bank is, like a cheque, an order to the banker to pay it. It is customary to *advise* bills payable at the London Agency, forms for which purpose are provided by all banks.

In Scotland, where a drawee of a bill has in his hands funds available for the payment thereof, the bill operates as an assignment of the sum for which it is drawn in favour of the holder from the time when the bill is presented to the drawee.

Interest can be recovered from the time of presentment for payment if the bill is payable on demand, and from the maturity of the bill in any other case.

A contemporaneous agreement that payment shall be postponed in no way controls the operation of a bill.

Where a bill has been protested for non-payment, any person may intervene and pay it *supra protest* for the honour of any party liable thereon, and the payer for honour has a right of recourse for repayment to the person for whose honour he paid, and to all parties to the bill who are liable to that person (see Acceptance, *supra protest*).

Renewals.

It frequently happens that when the acceptor is unable to meet the bill at maturity he applies for an extension of time, and a new bill is prepared in place of the old one. In such case the acceptor should be careful to cancel the old bill, and the holder to obtain the consent of other parties to the bill who are responsible to him. If a holder agrees with the acceptor to give him time to pay without the consent of the other parties responsible on the bill, the other parties are discharged from liability.

Consideration.

Valuable consideration is presumed to have been given for a bill, and it is for the party liable thereon to prove that no consideration was given. Valuable consideration for a bill may be constituted by an antecedent debt or liability, or any consideration sufficient to support a simple contract. A holder who has a lien on the bill is deemed a holder for value to the extent of the sum for which he has a lien.

Where the holder has given no consideration for a bill he cannot enforce payment, but if he pays over the bill to another person and receives value therefor that person can recover on the bill.

Accommodation Bills.

An accommodation party to a bill is a person who has signed a bill as drawer, acceptor, or indorser without receiving value therefor, and for the purpose of lending his name to some other person. An accommodation party is liable on the bill to a holder for value, and it is immaterial whether when such holder took the bill he knew such party to be an accommodation party or not.

Accommodation acceptances are frequently exchanged, a practice which is the source of much commercial immorality.

Holder in Due Course.

A " holder in due course," or a " *bona-fide* holder for value without notice," is a holder who has taken a bill complete and regular on the face of it under the following conditions:—(i.) That he became the holder of it before it was overdue and without notice that it had been previously dishonoured, if such was the fact; (ii.) That he took the bill in good faith and for value, and that at the time the bill was negotiated to him he had no notice of any defect in the title of the person who negotiated it.

The title of a person who negotiates a bill is defective when he obtained the bill, or the acceptance thereof, by fraud, duress, or force and fear, or for illegal consideration.

Capacity of Parties, Signature, Stamp, &c.

Any person capable of entering into a contract is also capable of becoming party to a bill.

A signature by *procuration* operates as notice that the agent has but a limited authority to sign, and the principal is only bound by such signature if the agent in so signing was acting within the actual limits of his authority.

Where a person signs a bill, and adds words to his signature indicating that he signs for or on behalf of a principal, or in a representative character, he is not personally liable thereon.

An *Agent* who signs without authority is liable to an action for damages.

An Agent or representative should either sign by procuration signature, or prefix words to his signature specifying that he signs for or on behalf of his principal.

Thus—

For the Blanktown Woollen Co., Ld.,
Benj. Broadbent,
Secretary.

The full ordinary signature of the signer for procuration should be given, and not the bare initials.

A signature to a bill or promissory note need not be in the handwriting of the person required to sign same, but it is sufficient if his name be written thereon by some other person by or under his authority.

In the case of a Corporation the Corporation Seal is sufficient, although the seal is not necessary if the bill be otherwise signed.

Bills and promissory notes must be stamped with an impressed stamp before the execution thereof.

The penalty for issuing an unstamped bill or note is £1o.

Bills of Exchange payable on demand, or at sight, or on presentation are subject to a uniform duty of one penny, which may be affixed by an adhesive stamp.

The stamps required for all other Inland Bills and promissory notes, are as follows:—

Where the amount or value of the money for which the bill or note is drawn or made does not

Exceed £5 o o 1

Exceeds £5 and does not exceed £1o.. . oo2 11 £TM ,, ,, £25... oo3 .. £25 .. , £5-oo6

£50 .. £75 -oo9

,, £75 ,, ,, £1oo... o 1 o

,, £1oo, for every £1oo and also for any fractional part of "1oo... o1o

Foreign and Colonial Bills.

Foreign Bills are usually drawn in sets of two or three, all of the same tenor and date (see example, p. 286), the several parts being transmitted by different routes as security against accidents or delays.

The first of the set that comes to hand being accepted the other parts are of course useless.

Acceptance may be written on any one part, and it must be written on *one part only.* If a drawee accepts more than one part, or if a holder indorses more than one part, he is liable on every such part so accepted or indorsed that gets into the hands of different holders in due course (see also *Acceptance,* page 288).

Where the acceptor of a bill drawn in a set pays it without requiring the part bearing his acceptance to be delivered up to him, and that part at maturity is outstanding in the hands of a holder in due course, he his liable to the holder thereof.

Bills are usually drawn in the currency of the place where they are payable, and the sum to be paid is calculated at the rate of exchange *(g* for demand drafts at the place where the bill is payable on the day it is due. Bills drawn payable *exchange per endorsement,* entitle the holder to negotiate the bill before it becomes due at the current rate of exchange on the date of negotiation, the acceptor undertaking to pay accordingly. Any difference between the rate of exchange on the date of negotiation and the rate of exchange on the date when the bill matures is usually adjusted between the payer and payee, and is either part of the contract for which payment is made or is allowed in account current.

Bills drawn in the United Kingdom on merchants in India and the Colonies are frequently negotiated through banks having agencies in the place where the merchant resides. The bills of lading and shipping documents relating to the goods in respect of which the bills are drawn are hypothecated to the bank as security. In this way payment for goods can be obtained, less the cost of discount and exchange, immediately the goods are shipped, without risk to the shipper, as the bank's agent will not hand over the bill of lading until the bill of exchange is honoured.

(g) For explanation as to the term "Bate of Exohange," refer to any good encyclopedia, where not only the explanation bat also the titles of works dealing with the subject more fully may be found

A foreign bill must be stamped on its being received in this country, to the same amount as if it were an inland bill; but the stamp may be an adhesive foreign bill stamp.

CHEQUES.

A Cheque is a bill of exchange drawn on a banker, payable on demand, and the law applicable to a bill of exchange on demand generally applies to a cheque.

A cheque should be *immediately presented for payment,* and a person who takes a stale cheque takes it at his peril.

Notice of dishonour must be given to the drawer and indorser, if any.

The duty and authority of a banker to pay a cheque drawn on him by his customer, are determined by countermand of payment, notice of the customer's death, or knowledge that the customer has committed an act of bankruptcy.

Subject to the preceding paragraph, if a banker, having sufficient funds in hand, dishonours his customer's cheque he is liable to him in an action for damages.

A cheque *crossed,* by drawing across its face two parallel lines and writing " & Co." between, is payable to a banker only. If a cheque is crossed *specially* by writing the name of a banker across its face it is payable only to the banker specified.

Cheques should be so written that they cannot be tampered with or altered. A carelessly drawn cheque for, say, £8 : 1o: o (eight pounds ten shillings), might easily be altered to *£8o* : 1o: o (eighty pounds ten shillings), and the possibility of such fraudulent substitution of a larger amount should therefore be prevented.

The indorsement across the cheque of words such as " under twenty pounds " is a very common safeguard.

Letters of Credit.

A Letter of Credit is an authority from one banker to another to pay money to another person.

VIII. INFORMATION ON MERCANTILE SUBJECTS.

It is very desirable that a book-keeper should be fully alive to all customs, regulations, and legal requirements connected with the affairs of the counting-house. He should be prepared to act promptly on emergency, although careful to seek proper advice upon matters of difficulty or uncertainty. The following information relates to a few of those subjects with which every efficient book-keeper should be thoroughly acquainted:—

Bills of Lading.

A Bill of Lading is an acknowledgment, on stamped paper, given by the master of a vessel for goods received on board, containing also an agreement as to their delivery, freight, &c. Three copies are made A sixpenny stamp, impressed before execution is required. out—two for the use of the shipper and one for the master. The Bill of Lading gives a right to the holder to receive the goods, and, like a Bill of Exchange, may be negotiated by being indorsed over to another person.

Guaranty and Collateral Security.

When a customer's account becomes larger than his apparent means warrant, either a guaranty or collateral security is frequently obtained.

A GUARANTY is a promise to answer for the payment of a debt, or the performance of a duty, in the case of the failure of a person who is himself, in the first instance, liable to such payment or performance. A guaranty cannot be enforced unless it is in writing. A person who has given a guaranty is discharged if the holder of the guaranty agrees to give time to the principal without his consent, and, generally, if he substitutes any other agreement with the principal which alters the situation of the surety, or differs from that for the performance of which the surety is responsible. A guaranty is not valid unless there be some consideration given therefor.

COLLATERAL SECURITY is security given in addition to the chief security. It is frequently given to a banker to secure the overdraft of a customer, and in the event of the bankruptcy of the customer the bank has the right to claim on the customer's estate for the full amount of his debt and then to have recourse to the collateral security, the giver of the collateral security having no remedy.

Interest.

Interest may be charged upon debts payable by virtue of some written instrument at a *certain* time. In other cases interest can be claimed only from the date when a demand for payment shall have been made, in writing, giving notice that interest will be claimed. Forms for invoices and statements should therefore intimate that interest will be charged on overdue accounts.

Lien.

Lien is a right to retain property until a debt due to the person retaining has been satisfied. There are two species of liens known as *Particular* and *General. Particular* liens are where persons claim to retain the goods in respect of which the debt arises; as where a Dyer has a lien on goods delivered to him to dye.

General liens are claimed in respect of a general balance of account. They are very strictly construed by the courts, and will not be allowed unless proved upon strong evidence, such as express contract, or the usage of trade. It is customary, therefore, for Dyers, Finishers, and other Commission Workers to print an express stipulation for a general lien on their invoices and statements.

Statute of Frauds, Contracts over £10.

The Statute of Frauds enacts that no contract for the sale of any goods for the price of £10 and upwards shall be allowed to be good, except the buyer shall accept pan of the goods so sold, and actually receive same, or give something in earnest to bind the bargain, or in part payment, or that some note or memorandum in writing of the said bargain be made and signed by the parties. The Act applies to goods to be delivered at some future time, as well as those to be delivered at once. It will therefore be seen that every order should, if possible, be obtained in writing, either directly or by admission.

Statutes of Limitation.

The Statutes of Limitation limit the time to six years within which an action may be brought to recover a debt, but a promise to pay, or an unqualified acknowledgment of the debt in writing, is sufficient to bar the Statute.

Stoppage in Transitu.

When goods are consigned on credit and the consignee becomes insolvent before the goods arrive the important right or privilege of stoppage *in transitu* may be exercised. The consignor of the goods may direct the carrier to return the goods to him. The right of stoppage in transit may sometimes be defeated, as where the consignee of the goods indorses the bill of lading to a *bom fide* indorsee (see Bills of Lading).

I N DEX.

ACCEPTANCE, see *Bills of Exchange*
  Account Current, interest on, 216
  Accounts, fictitious, impersonal, real, note *d*, 8
nominal, personal, property, 8,13,16,16
opening in ledger, 11, 06, 66
quarterly or periodical, treated as invoices, 198
  Agents, deducting commission, 206
  Allowances, see *Returns and Allowances*
  Alphabetical Index to ledgers, 274, 276
  Audit, advantages of, 280, 281
BAD DEBTS Account, 216
composition, promissory notes, 206, 208
customer's account, 206
provision fund, note s, 216
separate ledger for, note a, 216
Balance, see *Trial Balance*
Book, Set I., 73—76, Set II., 209
left over in settlement, 204
Sheet 17, Set I., 77—80, Set II., 211
Balk Book, 263, 266, 267
Bank Account, how to balance, 63, 64
charges, 70, 218
terms, 238
cashier's duties in respect of, 238
pass book, note il, 63
Bills Of Exchange, 286—294
acceptance, 288
accommodation bills, 291
alterations, incompleteness, irregularity, 287
capacity of parties, 292
consideration, 291
definitions, 287
dishonour, notice of, 289, 290
foreign and colonial, 293
forms, 286
bolder in due course, 292
interest on, 291
may be payable in instalments, 287
  Bills Of Exchange (continued)
negotiation and indorsement, 287, 288
noting and protest, 290
payment and rights of holder, 290, 291
presentment for payment, 289
renewals, 291
signature, stamp, 292
stamps on, 292, 293, 294
Bills of Lading, 294, 296
Bills Ledgers, Set I., 68-70, Set II., 207, 208
  Payable, 12, 13, Set I., 69, Set II., 207
Receivable, 12, 13, Set I., 69, 70, Set II., 207, 208
bank discount on, 70
discounted, not by bank, 208
dishonoured, (customer's account), 206
renewed, (customer's accnt.) 207, 208
  Book File, for invoices, note *a* 67
for credit notes (sales) note/, 69
for cash vouchers, 64
Butldtngs, repairs to, 214
new erections, 214
see also *Depreciation*
CANVAS returned, 200
Capital Account, 6, 7, 11, 17, Set I., 77—80
Set II., 216
manipulation of, see *Finance*
Cards Account, 214, 216
trade discount on, 214
see also *Depreciation*
Carriage paid by firm, reclaimable, 203
Cash Book, Set I., 60—66, Set II., 201, 202
another form of, 231, 232
how to balance, 63
Cashier's Duties, 238—240
Charges paid for customer, 206
Cheques, 294
customer's, 206
dishonored, 206
Claim Notes, note/, 69
Claims, see *Returns and Claims*
Classification—
of expenditure, see *Trading Account*
of orders, 262
of purchases, 67, 198
of transactions, 21, 277, see also *Test Journal*
  Collateral Security, 294
  Combers, see *Commission Workers*
  Commission, deducted by agent, 206
workers, speoial books, 227
  Composition to Creditors, 206
promissory notes for, 208, see also *Bad Debts*
  Consignment Stock Books, 266, 270, 271
  Contra Entries, bank and cash, 61
accounts, how to deal with, 204, 204
  Contracts, over £10, 296, 296
  Cost Books, see *Mill and Factory Books,*
246—271
  Country Work, 199, and see *Outwork*
  Credit, creditor, 7—9
  Notes, (purchases) note *c,* 68
  (sales) note/, 69
  Customer's bills and cheques, 206, 208
DAMAGES, shorts and allowances, see *Returns and Allowances*
  Date for payment, special, 204
  Day Book, see *Purchases, Sales, Mill Sales,*
and *Returns, die..* Day Books
  Debit, debtor, 7—9
  Decimal Calculations, 226
  Delivery Notes, 198, 227
  Departmental Accounts, 219 —224
  Departments, record of work done in, 266, 267
  Depreciation, how entered, 79, 216

principles and measure of oharge, 233 237
table, 236
Detail Lehger, 228
Discounting, see *Finance*
Discounts, how entered, 60, 78, 216, 218
Dishonourtm bill, 206
cheque, 206
Dividends, see *Bad Debts*
Double Entry, 8
advantages of, 6
Dyers, see *Commission Workers*
ENTRY, separate book of, 22, 28
Entrtes to agree with postings 14, and see *I'est Journal*
Engineers And Machinists, Detail Ledger
suitable for, 228
Errors—
in balancing, how discovered and avoided, 278—280
in remittance, 204
localised, see *Test Journal*
FACTORY or Mill Books, 246—271
Fictitious Accounts, note *d*, 8
Finance, 238—240
Finishers, see *Commission Workers*
GAS Account, 78, 218
Goods Account, 11, 16, 17
combined in Trading Account, 26, note *n*, 211
Delivered Book, 227
Received Book, 227
purchased, see *Purchases Day Book*
returned, see *Returns, etc., Day Books*
sold, see *Sales Day Book*
Guaranty, 296
HORSES and vehicles, account of, 213
IMPERSONAL ACCOUNTS, note *d*, 8
Inctdental Expenses, 214
Incomb Tax, 281—286
account, 216
Index to Ledger, 274, 276
Insolvent Account, 206, see *Bad Debts*
Insurance Account, 78, 213
Interest, 296
calculations, 277, 278
on account current, 216
on capital, a charge against the Trading Account, 79
on overdue accounts, not claimable without notice, note *m*, 240, 296
on partners' drawings, 216
on personal accounts, 203

Invoices for purchases, see *Purchatu Day Book*
for sales, see *Sales Day Book*
JOURNAL, 21—23, note *t*, 216 and see *Test Journal*
LEASES, see *Depreciation*
Ledger, its divisions —for postings only—66
alphabetical index to, 274, 276
detail, 228—230
opening, indexing, and ruling off accounts, 66, 66
see also *Purchases, Sales, Bills, Nominal* and *Private* Ledgers
Letter of Credit, 294
Lien, 296
Loan Accounts, 216
interest on, 216
MACHINERY Account, see *Plant,* and see *Depreciation,* 233—237
or Manufacturing Profit or Lobs, see *Departmental Accounts,* also 268
Manufacturing: Departments, 219—224
Mill Furnishinos, Ac, Account, 213, see also *Departmental Accounts*
Mill Ledger, see *Purchases Ledger*
Mill or Factory and Warehouse Books, 246—271.
Mill Sales Day Book, 199
Motive Power Account, 212
NOMINAL Aocounts, 8, 13, 16
Ledger, 209, 211, 215
Noting, see *Bills of Exchange,* 290
OPENING account in Ledger, 11, 66, 66
Ohder Book, at Mill for purchases, 247
for piece goods, 261, 266
at Warehouse, 264, 270
Onders Making Classification Book, 262, 266, 267
Outwork, 220 and note x, 222
Overcharge, 203
PACKING MATERIAL, note *y,* 222
Partners' Drawings, 79
interest on, 216
must pay for purchases from the firm, 207
Pattern Day Book, 200

making, cost of, 220, and note a, 223
Personal Accounts, 8, 16
Petty Cash, or Petty Expenses Book, 64, 202
Piece Cost Book, 264
makiug, or Balk Book, 263, 266, 267
Order Book at Mill, 261
workers, see *Wages*
Plant and Machinery Account, 79, 216
see also *Depreciation*
Posting, 66
postings to agree with entries 14, and see *Test Journal*
to which ledger, 210
Power Account, 212, note *i,* 223
Private Drawings, see *Partners' Drawings*
Private Ledger, Set I., 71—73, Set II., 216, 216
what posted thereto, 72, 216, 216
Profit and Loss, how ascertained, 16
account, combined in Trading Account, note *n,* 211
definition of, note *n,* 211
Promissory Notes, 286, 287
stamps on, 292, 293
see *Composition,* 208
Property Accounts, 8, 16
Protest, see *Bills of Exchange*
Provision Fund, see *Bad Debts*
Purchases and Sales to same party, 203, 204
Day Book, Set I., 67, Set II., 198
Ledger, Set I., 66, 67, Set II., 202-204
what posted thereto, 66, 67, 210
small, ledger account of, 204
RATES, Ac, Account, 213
Real Accounts, note *d,* 8
Receipts, see *Vouchers,* 64, 66
Renewed Bill, 207, 208, 291
Rent, *Ac,* Account, 78, 213
Repairs and Renewals to Machinery, 213
to Buildings, 214
Returns and Allowances (Sales) Day Book
Set I., 69, Set II., 200
and Allowances Book File, note /, 69
column for small claims iu cash book, 201
and Claims (Purchases) Day Book, Set I., 68, Set II., 198, on dyers and fin-

ishers, 68
   Room and Power, 212, note f, 223
SALARIES, travellers', 214
warehouse and office, 214
   Sales and purchases from same party, 203,
204
at Mill, 199
ledger account of, 204
   Day Rook, Set I., 68, 69, Set II., 200
   Lodger, Set I., 08, Set II., 204—207
what posted thereto, 68, 210
for season's goods, 230, 231
to partners, 207
   Security, collateral, 296
   Selling departments, 219
profit, 221
   Separate books of entry, 22, 28
   Settlement, how to distinguish items comprised in, 206
   Shorts, see *Returnt and Allowancet*
   Special dates for payment, 204
terms for payment, 206
   Spinners, see *Committion Workera*
detail ledger, 228—230
skeps and bobbins, 228—230, see also

note *q,* 213
   Stables Account, 213
   Statute of Frauds, 296, 296
of Limitations, 296
8tock Books, see *Mill or Factory and Ware-*
house Books, 246—271
Stock-takino, 269, 260
Stoppage in *transitu,* 296
Sundry Persons Account, 204, 207
TARE records, 228
Taxes Account, 213
see *Income Tax*
   Terms of payment, special, 206
should be printed on invoice and statement forms, 240
   Test Journal, Set I., 76, 77, Set II., 210,
211
   Timeeeppkh, see *Wages*
   Timeworkers, see *Wages*
   Tiurnco Account, 26, 77—80, 211—218
arrangement of 217
definition of, note n, 211
how treated, 16

see *Departmental Accounts*
Transfers, 211
   Travellers' salaries and expenses, 214
results compared, note r, 214
   Trial Balance, 14, 20, 74, see also *Balance*
Book
different methods of preparing, 276, 277
   Turnino, see *Motive Power*
VOLUME and value of production, 226
Vouchers, see *Cash Book,* 60, 64, 66
WAGES, 212, 241—246, see also *Salaries*
book, 64
Warehouse Books, 246—271
Waste, sales of, 199
Weaveh's Ticket, 263, 268
Weight Notes, 138
Work Done, record of, 266, 267
summary of, 268
YARN, see *Spinner*
shade register, 262, 268
ALFRED JUBB & SON, LTD., PRINTERS. HUDDERSFIELD.